D1576861

ARRABAL: PLAYS VOLUME THREE

The Spanish-born playwright and novelist Fernando Arrabal is
one of the most controversial figures in the contemporary French
theatre. His provocative and original creative intelligence explores
human reality and fantasy with brilliant insight, which often shocks
and always fascinates. Symbols and erotic fantasies play a large
part in all these plays which beside being effective on stage make
thought-provoking and enjoyable reading.

The Architect and the Emperor of Assyria is a brilliant and
disturbing play vividly depicting the sexual perversions and
deviations in a relationship between two men on a desert island.

The Grand Ceremonial is, perhaps, Arrabal's weirdest play yet
strangely poetic and utterly compelling. The play's central
relationship between the cripple Cavanosa and his lover Sil reaches
the heights of bizarrerie and imaginatively shows the extent of the
characters' emotional, as well as physical, sickness. Both these
plays have been successfully produced all over Europe and The
Grand Ceremonial has been filmed as The Weird Weirdo.

The Solemn Communion, a short play, tellingly contrasts a young
girl preparing for her first communion with a necrophile violating
a corpse. The ritual elements of both acts combine to create a
powerful theatrical image. The play has already been successfully
presented in this translation at the Soho Lunchtime Theatre in
April 1970.

The translator of the first two plays, Jean Benedetti, is well-known
as a director in the theatre and is currently Principal of The Rose
Bruford College, one of the country's leading drama schools.
John Calder's translation of The Solemn Communion has already
appeared in the quarterly theatre magazine Gambit, published
by Calder and Boyars.

arrabal

THE ARCHITECT AND THE EMPEROR OF ASSYRIA
THE GRAND CEREMONIAL
THE SOLEMN COMMUNION

plays volume 3

TRANSLATED BY
JEAN BENEDETTI & JOHN CALDER

CALDER AND BOYARS · LONDON

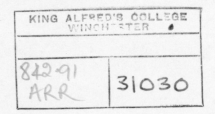

Printed by photo-lithography
and made in Great Britain at
The Pitman Press, Bath.

CONTENTS

THE ARCHITECT AND
THE EMPEROR OF ASSYRIA

CHARACTERS

THE EMPEROR OF ASSYRIA

THE ARCHITECT

ACT ONE

Scene One

(The sound of aeroplanes.
The ARCHITECT looks for a place to hide like a hunted
frightened animal. He runs in all directions; burrows in
the earth; starts running again and finally buries his head
in the sand.
Explosion. The glow of flames.
The ARCHITECT, his head still half buried in the sand,
sticks his fingers in his ears and trembles with fear.
A few moments later the EMPEROR enters. He has a sort
of stilted elegance. He is trying to maintain his composure.
He taps the "other" with the end of his walking stick and
says:)

EMPEROR. My dear sir, kindly telephone. I am the only
survivor from the crash.

ARCHITECT. (Horrified) Fi! Fi! Figa! Figa! Fi! Fi!

(He stares at the EMPEROR for a moment completely
shattered then runs out as fast as he can.)

Scene Two

(Two years later.
On stage the EMPEROR and the ARCHITECT.)

EMPEROR. It's really very simple. Try again.

ARCHITECT. (He has a little trouble pronouncing the 's')
Escalator.

EMPEROR. (Forcefully) Two years I've been living on this
island! Two years I've been giving you lessons and still
you hesitate. I think Aristotle would have to rise from the
grave to teach you the sum of two tables and two chairs.

9

ARCHITECT. I've learned how to talk haven't I?

EMPEROR. Well .... yes. At least if anyone should stumble on this remote island you'll be able to say "Ave Caesar".

ARCHITECT. Today you said you'd teach me ....

EMPEROR. Now harken to my muse that sings the anger of Achilles. My throne!

(The EMPEROR sits. The ARCHITECT bows down before him.)

That's right. That's right. Don't forget that I am the Emperor of Assyria.

ARCHITECT. Assyria is bounded on the North by the Caspian Sea and in the South by the Indian Ocean ....

EMPEROR. You needn't go on.

ARCHITECT. Teach me - you promised - about ....

EMPEROR. Gently, gently. Ah! (Dreamily) Civilisation, civilisation!

ARCHITECT. (Happily) Yes, yes.

EMPEROR. Be quiet. What do you know about it? You've spent your life on an island that's not even mentioned on the map, shat by God into the ocean in a moment of contempt.

ARCHITECT. Tell me, tell me!

EMPEROR. On your knees.

(The ARCHITECT kneels.)

That's right, and quite unnecessary.

(The ARCHITECT rises.)

EMPEROR. (Forcefully) I shall explain!

ARCHITECT. Oh, yes do!

EMPEROR. Be quiet. (Once again: Forcefully) I shall explain ....
my life. (He rises. With grand gestures) I rose at dawn's

first glimmer. Churches, synagogues and temples would sound their trumpets. Day was breaking. My father came to wake me with a regiment of violins. Ah! Music. Ah! How wonderful. (Suddenly anxious) Have you cooked the sausages and mash?

ARCHITECT. Yes sire.

EMPEROR. Where was I? Ah, yes, being awakened by the regiment of trumpets that used to come in the morning and the church violins .... What mornings they were! What a way to wake up! Then beautiful, blind slave-women would come to teach me philosophy. Ah, philosophy! One day I'll tell you what that is.

ARCHITECT. Sire, how did they teach you philosophy?

EMPEROR. There's no need to go into details. And my fiancee .... and my mother ....

ARCHITECT. Mummy, mummy, mummy.

EMPEROR. (Terrified) Where did you hear that cry?

ARCHITECT. You taught it me.

EMPEROR. When! Where?

ARCHITECT. The other day.

EMPEROR. What did I say?

ARCHITECT. You said that your mother used to take you in her arms and rock you and that she used to kiss you on the forehead and that ....

(The EMPEROR visualises the scene that is being described. He curls up in his chair as though some invisible person were rocking him, kissing him etc.......)

.... and you said that sometimes she used to beat you with a whip and that she used to take your hand when you were out walking in the street and that ....

EMPEROR. Stop! Stop! Is the fire alight?

ARCHITECT. Yes.

EMPEROR. You're sure it stays alight day and night?

11

ARCHITECT. Yes, look at the smoke.

EMPEROR. That's good. What's the point?

ARCHITECT. What do you mean, what's the point? You
said one day a ship or an aeroplane might see us and come
towards us.

EMPEROR. And then what will we do?

ARCHITECT. Well, we'll go to your country where there are cars
and television and women and plates of confetti and ideas
by the square mile and Thursdays longer than God made
and . . . .

EMPEROR. (Changing the subject) Have you prepared the cross?

ARCHITECT. There it is. (He points to the brushwood) Are you
going to crucify me now?

EMPEROR. What? Are you the one that's to be crucified? Not
me?

ARCHITECT. We drew lots. Don't you remember?

EMPEROR. (Angrily) I don't believe it! We drew lots to decide
who was to redeem mankind?

ARCHITECT. Master, you can't remember a thing.

EMPEROR. And how did we draw lots for it? What with?

ARCHITECT. With a length of straw.

(The EMPEROR has a fit of giggles repeating over and
over again "a length, a length".)

ARCHITECT. Master, what are you laughing at?

EMPEROR. You're taking a lot on yourself, aren't you? Being
very familiar?

ARCHITECT. You said . . . .

EMPEROR. I never told you what the word length means, slip
a length.

ARCHITECT. You said we were friends. Are we or not?

12

EMPEROR. Blind women who taught me philosophy dressed only in a pink bath towel. I have a wonderful memory. I can remember it as if it were yesterday. How they caressed my divine body. How they would clean its grubbiest corners .... To horse!

ARCHITECT. Shall I be the horse?

EMPEROR. No, me !

> (The EMPEROR gets down on all fours.
> The ARCHITECT sits astride him.)

EMPEROR. Say, Gee up!

ARCHITECT. Gee up, Neddy!

EMPEROR. Whip me with the riding crop!

> (The ARCHITECT beats him with a branch.)

ARCHITECT. Gee up, Neddy! Faster! We're on our way to Babylon! Faster! Gee up!

> (They trot round the stage several times.)

> (Suddenly the EMPEROR throws him down.)

EMPEROR. (In a blind fury) You're not wearing spurs! What do you mean by it?

ARCHITECT. What are spurs?

EMPEROR. How do you expect us to get to ....

ARCHITECT. Babylon.

EMPEROR. (Afraid) Where did you get that word? Who taught it you? Who's been coming to see you while I'm asleep?

> (He throws himself on the ARCHITECT and half strangles him.)

ARCHITECT. You taught it me.

EMPEROR. I did?

ARCHITECT. Yes, you said it was a city in your Empire in Assyria.

(The EMPEROR regains control of himself. Forcefully:)

EMPEROR. Ants!

(He watches a procession of ants on the ground.)

Ants! Little slaves! Go and fetch me a cup of water immediately.

(He sits on his throne and waits. Anxiously:)

Did you hear me?

(Long silence.)

I said go and fetch me a cup of water.

(Furious:)

What! Is there no respect for the EMPEROR OF ASSYRIA? Can such things be? Then die at my feet!

(He rushes furiously to the ants and crushes them under foot.
He falls exhausted onto his "throne".)

ARCHITECT. Here.

EMPEROR. (Knocking the cup away) What do you want me to do with water? I only drink vodka. (He giggles)

ARCHITECT. Didn't you say that . . . .

EMPEROR. And my fiancee? Did I tell you about my fiancee?

ARCHITECT. (As though he were reciting a lesson) She-was-very-pretty-very-beautiful-very-fair-with-green-eyes-and . . . .

EMPEROR. Are you taking the mickey?

ARCHITECT. You told me about her already.

EMPEROR. Do you want to be my fiancee?

ARCHITECT. Now?

EMPEROR. Are you refusing to be my fiancee? (Furious)
Beast!

14

ARCHITECT. I'm always the girl these days and you do fuck-all.

EMPEROR. Now I've taught you to swear. It's the end.

ARCHITECT. When are you going to teach me architecture.

EMPEROR. What for? You're an architect already, aren't you?

ARCHITECT. All right, I'll be the girl.

EMPEROR. I thought you just said you wanted me to teach you
  about architecture? Ah, architecture!

ARCHITECT. We were saying that I was to be the girl.

EMPEROR. We were saying that I was going to teach you about
  architecture today ...... the fundamentals of architecture
  ...... All right, I'll be the girl if you really want me to.

ARCHITECT. Well, what are the fundamentals of architecture?

EMPEROR. I said I'd be the girl today if-you-really-in-sist.

ARCHITECT. Put on your petticoats and skirts.

EMPEROR. I don't even know where they are. You lose everything. You leave things lying about. But ...... Do you
  really mean to tell me you don't know the fundamentals of
  architecture? You, an Assyrian architect? Do you really
  mean to say that you have stooped to such deception that I
  made you Grand Architect of Assyria when you don't even
  know the rudiments of architecture? What will the neigh-
  bours say?

ARCHITECT. You gave me the title. It's not my fault. I'm not
  an Emperor.

EMPEROR. Where are those damned skirts? Ants! Go and fetch
  my petticoats and skirts immediately!

ARCHITECT. They won't do it.

EMPEROR. What do you mean they won't do it? Ants, slaves, go
  and fetch my skirts, I'm playing the girl today ...... Do
  you hear me? But ...... where's my head? I forgot.
  I've just squashed them all ...... (Very quietly) Listen,
  be honest with me, do you think I'm a dictator?

ARCHITECT. What's a dictator?

EMPEROR. Of course, I'm no soldier. Tell me, my subjects, are you oppressed by my yoke? Tell me, confess, am I a tyrant?

ARCHITECT. Are you going to put these skirts on or not?

EMPEROR. I'm asking you if I am a tyrant?

ARCHITECT. You're not a tyrant. (Angry) Satisfied?

EMPEROR. I have slain the ants! Tyrants . . . . . .

ARCHITECT. The skirts!

EMPEROR. Are we playing priests today?

ARCHITECT. All right, I can see you don't feel like it today.

EMPEROR. (Without putting on the skirts he becomes a woman. A woman's voice.) "Oh, my love, do you love me? Together we will go . . . . . ."

ARCHITECT. "You are so beautiful that when I think of you I feel a flower growing between my legs and its transparent bloom covers my thighs . . . . . . May I touch your knees?"

EMPEROR. (Woman) I have never been so happy. Such joy wells up in me that fountains spring from my hands to your hands. "

ARCHITECT. "You, with your soft white round knees. "

EMPEROR. (Woman) "Stroke them. "

(The EMPEROR tries to raise his trouser leg to show his knee but he cannot.)

EMPEROR. Blast! The skirts! (Silence)

ARCHITECT. I've built a canoe.

EMPEROR. Are you going? Are you going to leave me alone?

ARCHITECT. I'll paddle until I reach the shore of another island.

EMPEROR. (Emphatically) Oh! Fortunate young man. Homer was the herald of your virtues.

ARCHITECT. What?

EMPEROR. And your mother?

16

ARCHITECT. I didn't have a mother, you know that!

EMPEROR. You are the son of a siren and a centaur. The perfect match! (Very sad) Mummy, mummy.

> (He takes a few steps looking for her. He looks under the throne.)

> Mummy where are you? It's me. I'm all alone here, they've all forgotten me, but you ....

ARCHITECT. (Has put on a veil: he plays the mother) What's the matter, child? You're not alone, mummy's here.

EMPEROR. Mummy, everybody hates me, they've left me alone on this island.

ARCHITECT. (very maternal: protects him covering him with his arms) No, child. I'm here to protect you. You mustn't feel lonely. Tell your mother everything.

EMPEROR. Mummy, the architect's going to leave me. He's built a canoe and he'll go away and I'll be left all alone here.

ARCHITECT. (Mother) That's not true. It's for your own good. You'll see. He's going to look for help and then they'll come back and save you.

EMPEROR. Are you sure Mummy?

ARCHITECT. (Mother) Yes, child.

EMPEROR. Mummy, don't go away. Stay with me always.

ARCHITECT. (Mother) Yes, child. I'll stay here with you, night and day.

EMPEROR. Darling, Mummy, kiss me.

> (The ARCHITECT leans towards him to give him a kiss. The EMPEROR pushes him away brutally.)

EMPEROR. You stink! You stink! What the hell have you been eating?

ARCHITECT. The same as you.

EMPEROR. Make an appointment to see the dentist. Have

your teeth filled. You give off a filthy smell.

ARCHITECT. You promised me ....

EMPEROR. I promised you, I promised you .... so what?

Bring me my box of cigars.

ARCHITECT. (Bowing low) May your Majesty's will be done.

(He goes out and returns with a stone.)

ARCHITECT. Here they are, sir.

(The EMPEROR touches the stone, pretends to select a
good cigar, takes it; sniffs it; cuts the end.)

EMPEROR. Ah! An aroma fit for the gods! Ah! Genevieve and
Michael cigars!

(The ARCHITECT pretends to light the cigar with a
lighter.)

ARCHITECT. Light, sir?

EMPEROR. With a lighter? You must have studied valeting at
the University of .... How frightful! The service is
deplorable! With a match .... Where have you left the
canoe?
ARCHITECT. On the beach.

EMPEROR. (Very sad) When did you make it? (Not giving him
time to reply) You built it without breathing a word to me.
Why? Swear you won't leave without telling me.

ARCHITECT. I swear.

EMPEROR. On what?

ARCHITECT. On anything you like, on all that's most sacred.

EMPEROR. On the Constitution of the Island.

ARCHITECT. I thought this was an absolute monarchy?

EMPEROR. Silence! I and I alone shall speak here.

ARCHITECT. When are you going to tell me about it?

18

EMPEROR. What are you talking about? You spend the whole bloody day twittering on will I tell you about it, will I tell you about it.

ARCHITECT. You promised me that today you'd teach me how to be happy.

EMPEROR. Not now. Later - really.

ARCHITECT. That's what you always say.

EMPEROR. Do you doubt my word?

ARCHITECT. What's it like being happy?

EMPEROR. I'll tell you about it. So impatient, so impatient. Ah! Youth!

ARCHITECT. Do you know how I imagine it to be? I think that when you're happy, you're with someone who has a very delicate skin and then you kiss them and everything is veiled in a pink mist and the person's body changes into a host of little mirrors and when you look at her you're reflected millions of times and you walk with her on zebras and panthers by a lake and she has got you on a rope and when you look at her it rains dove's feathers which neigh like young colts as they fall to the ground and then you go into a room and you start walking on the ceiling hand in hand .... (He speaks rapidly) and the heads are covered with snakes and the snakes are covered with bear-skins which tickle and the bear-skins are covered with gold, full of presents and golden scarabs ....

EMPEROR. Enough!

ARCHITECT. Mooo! Mooo!

(He goes down on all fours)

Look, I'm a cow.

EMPEROR. Shut up, you're mad.

ARCHITECT. Masturbate me?

EMPEROR. Have you no respect for me?

ARCHITECT. You are the all illustrious, all wise Emperor of

all powerful Assyria.

(He bows very low several times)

EMPEROR. What did you dream today?

ARCHITECT. Assyria, which is the greatest empire of the
Western world in its struggle against the barbarians of the
Eastern world . . . .

EMPEROR. It's the other way round, you bloody idiot!

ARCHITECT. Shall I talk about the yellow peril?

EMPEROR. Have you gone reactionary?

ARCHITECT. Wasn't that right?

EMPEROR. Let's have a war.

(They prepare.
They crouch down: they seize "machine-guns": they fire.)

Ha-ha-ha-ha-ha-ha-

(They crawl on their stomachs:
They come face to face camouflaged:
Each has a "helmet" and a flag.)

ARCHITECT. (Camouflaged: you can only see his "flag") This
is Radio Victory.

(Announcer's voice) Enemy soldiers, don't be deceived by
the lying propaganda of your officers. This is the General
in chief speaking. Yesterday we exterminated half your
civilian population with hydrogen bombs. Surrender in uni-
form and you will have the right to military honours. For a
better world!

EMPEROR. (Same) This is the official station of New Radio
Victory. The Marshall in chief speaking. Enemy soldiers
do not be led astray by the demagogic utterance of your
superiors. Yesterday our rockets slaughtered your entire
civilian population, entire civilian population . . . .

(The needle is stuck.
The ARCHITECT leaves his camouflaged sector: he is
weeping.

The EMPEROR also leaves his sector, weeping.
They turn their backs to each other: they are dressed as
soldiers and "armed".
They weep as they look at photographs of dead civilians.
Suddenly they turn round, aim their guns and shout:)

ARCHITECT.)
EMPEROR.) Hands up, traitor!

(They throw down their machine-guns raise their hands;
look at each other very frightened: then:)

ARCHITECT. Are you an enemy soldier?

EMPEROR. Don't kill me!

ARCHITECT. You neither.

EMPEROR. Is this the way you fight for a better world?

ARCHITECT. To tell you the truth I'm afraid of war. I'm crouched
right down in my trench, waiting, hoping that it will soon
be over.

EMPEROR. I put my hands up because of you. It's disgusting.
Fine soldiers you are, in the enemy army!

ARCHITECT. And what about you?

EMPEROR. I'm not much of a soldier. Here in my sector we all
want it to finish soon. What were you looking at in those
photos?

ARCHITECT. (Near to tears) All the members of my family
that you killed with your big bombs.

EMPEROR. (Condescendingly) Well, don't cry, old chap, look
at mine. You killed them.

ARCHITECT. Them too? We don't have much luck, do we? (He
bursts into tears)

EMPEROR. Do you mind if I cry with you?

ARCHITECT. All right ---- it's not a trick is it?

(They are both crying buckets.)

EMPEROR. (Majestically throws down his military equipment)
What a life I had. Every morning my father would come and
wake me with a retinue of ballerinas. They all danced for
me. Ah! The dance! One day I will teach you to dance.
Thanks to television the whole of Assyria could see my
levee. Then came the audiences. First there were the
civil audiences. I used to give them in bed while herma-
phrodite slaves combed me and poured all the perfumes of
Arabia over my body. Then we had the military audiences
which I used to give seated on my commode. Finally the
ecclesiastical audiences. (Anxiously) What is your religion?

ARCHITECT. The one you taught me.

EMPEROR. You believe in God then?

ARCHITECT. Want to baptise me?

EMPEROR. Good heavens haven't you been baptised? You're on
your way to perdition. You'll roast day and night for all
eternity. They will choose the most beautiful female
demons to excite you but they will insert red hot pokers in
your anus.

ARCHITECT. You told me I would go to heaven.

EMPEROR. You baby! How little you know of life.

ARCHITECT. Hear my confession.

(The EMPEROR sits on the throne.
The ARCHITECT prostrates himself at his knees.)

ARCHITECT. Father, I confess that I have . . . .

EMPEROR. What's this silly game we're playing? I'm being the
confessor again. Get out you cunning little hound. I won't
hear your confession. You shall die with the full weight of
your sins upon you and you will fry for all eternity and
all because of me.

ARCHITECT. I dreamed that . . . .

EMPEROR. Who asked to hear your dreams?

ARCHITECT. You did just now.

EMPEROR. Who cares about your dreams . . . . All right, let's hear them.

ARCHITECT. I dreamed I was alone on a desert island and
suddenly an aeroplane came down and I was in a panic, I
ran everywhere I was even trying to bury my head in the
sand when someone called me from behind ....

EMPEROR. Don't go on. What a strange dream. Help me, Freud!

ARCHITECT. Is it erotic too?

EMPEROR. Of course, what else?

ARCHITECT. (Bringing a whip) Going to beat me?

EMPEROR. (Condescending) All right. What part shall I play?

ARCHITECT. I don't mind.

EMPEROR. Shall I be your mother?

ARCHITECT. Come on, quick, beat me. I can't hold out much
longer.

(His back is bared: he is waiting for a few strokes of the
whip.)

EMPEROR. What's the meaning of this impatience? Now his lordship wants immediate service. Done as soon as said.

ARCHITECT. Come on, beat me. Just ten strokes. (Pleading)
Please!

EMPEROR. "Just" ten strokes. At my age! Who do you think I
am, young Hamlet, leaping over the graves of his polluting
ancestors?

ARCHITECT. Whip me, whip me. I can't hold out much longer,
it hurts me here.

EMPEROR. Come, come there's no need to be hysterical. I'll
whip you .... but .... how many times?

ARCHITECT. As many times as you like but be quick about it.
If you hit me really hard once it'll be enough.

EMPEROR. And where would his lordship like to be beaten.
(Emphatically) On his pink bottom, on his ebony back, on

his thighs, those elegiac columns of immortal Sparta?

ARCHITECT. Beat me! Beat me!

EMPEROR. All right, here goes!

> (Very solemnly, very slowly and very gently he hits him
> once: the whip hardly touches the skin.
> The ARCHITECT leaps at the EMPEROR, grabs the whip
> from him and beats himself twice very violently. He falls
> to the ground like a madman.
> Then he gets up and goes out.)

ARCHITECT. Goodbye for ever!

> (The EMPEROR walks up and down very decidedly.)

EMPEROR. All right then! Let's have something Shakespearean
- This is a good opportunity for a soliloquy.

> (He sobs: uses a large handkerchief to wipe his tears.)

Ah! Now I am alone!

> (Walks agitated)

How can I redeem humanity singlehanded?

> (He mimes the crucifixion, suddenly yells:)

Architect! Architect!

> (Quieter)

EMPEROR. Forgive me.

> (Weeps: uses handkerchief: mimes the crucifixion.)

The feet, yes. I can nail them better than the centurion
but . . . .

> (His gestures show that nailing the hands is a problem.)

Architect! . . . . come back, I'll whip you as many times
as you like.

> (He weeps.
> The ARCHITECT enters.

Very dignified, the EMPEROR stops weeping.)

How did you get there? Have you been listening at key-holes?
Have you been spying on me?

ARCHITECT. You're not angry?

EMPEROR. Shall I beat you?

ARCHITECT. There's no point.

EMPEROR. Have I ever told you about my fourteen secretaries?

ARCHITECT. The-fourteen-permanently-naked-secretaries-
who-wrote-down-the-masterpieces-you-dictated---

EMPEROR. How dare you poke fun at my writing. I was given a
Prize .... now what was it .... ?

ARCHITECT. The-Nobel-Prize-which-you-refused-because ....

EMPEROR. Be quiet, what do you know about ethics?

ARCHITECT. Ethics is bounded in the North by the Caspian
sea and in the South ....

EMPEROR. Thickhead! You're mixing it all up. That's Assyria.
Fancy confusing Assyria and Ethics. You savage! You
barbarian!

ARCHITECT. Shall I switch it off?

EMPEROR. Do what you like.

ARCHITECT. Le-lo-mil-loooo-looooo.

(The sky darkens as the ARCHITECT says these words:
night falls.)

VOICE OF THE EMPEROR. Trying to be funny again! I'm sick
of it. Make it day again. Bring back the light. I haven't
brushed my teeth yet.

VOICE OF THE ARCHITECT. You told me to do what I liked.

VOICE OF THE EMPEROR. Anything you like except make night
fall.

VOICE OF THE ARCHITECT. All right, here goes.

VOICE OF THE EMPEROR. Quickly.

VOICE OF THE ARCHITECT. Mi-ti-riiii-tiiiii!

(Daylight returns the same way it went.)

EMPEROR. And don't frighten me like that again.

ARCHITECT. I thought you wanted to sleep.

EMPEROR. That's none of your business. We have quite enough to do as it is. Let nature look after the sun and the moon.

ARCHITECT. Well, are you going to teach me philosophy?

EMPEROR. Philosophy? Me? (Sublimely) Philosophy! What a miracle. One day I will teach you this miracle of the human mind. This divine fruit of civilisation. (Anxiously) Tell me though, how do you make day and night.

ARCHITECT. Er! .... It's quite simple, really. I don't know how I do it.

EMPEROR. What about those words you were mumbling?

ARCHITECT. I just say them. I don't know why. But night would still fall even if I didn't use any words. I just have to wish.

EMPEROR. (Intrigued) And these words .... (Pulling himself up) Ignorant brute! You saw nothing! Have I told you about Television, Coca-Cola. Tanks, Babylonian museums, ministers, popes, the immensity of the ocean, the depth of our hypotheses ....

ARCHITECT. Tell me. Tell me.

EMPEROR. (Majestically sits on his throne) Bird. Yes, you sitting there on that branch, go and fetch me a haunch of venison immediately. Do you hear me? I am the Emperor of Assyria.

(He waits posing as a great Lord: anxiously.)

What? Do you dare rebel against my limitless power, my science, my sovereign eloquence, my word, my grandeur? I ordered you to go and fetch me a haunch of venison immediately.

(He waits. He picks up a stone and throws it at the branch.)

So be it, you shall die. I will only rule over obedient subjects.

ARCHITECT. Who will throw themselves at the feet of the most powerful Emperor in the West.

(He prostrates himself at the EMPEROR'S feet.)

EMPEROR. In the West? In the West and in the East. Don't you know that Assyria has already launched several manned satellites to Neptune? Tell me, do you know of any other achievement to equal that?

ARCHITECT. No one is more powerful in the whole beloved earth.

EMPEROR. Oh! My heart! .... The stretcher!

(The EMPEROR is twisted up with pain.
The ARCHITECT returns with a stretcher.)

My heart. Listen to it. I have a terrible stabbing pain. Ah, I have a weak heart.

(The ARCHITECT leans over the EMPEROR to listen to his heart.)

ARCHITECT. Don't worry, Emperor, I don't think it's anything. Rest and the pain will go away just as it has many times before.

EMPEROR. (Panting) No this time it's serious. I feel weak. I am sure it's a coronary thrombosis.

ARCHITECT. Your pulse is almost regular.

EMPEROR. Thank you my son, I know you're trying to put my mind at rest.

ARCHITECT. Have a little sleep and everything will be all right, you'll see.

EMPEROR. (Anxiously) My dying words? I've forgotten them. Tell me, tell me quickly, what were they?

ARCHITECT. I die and am content to die: I leave a world where all must perish and pass into eternity. But don't worry

27

about that.

EMPEROR. I want to tell you a secret, something I've never
told you before. When I die I want to be disguised. (Pause)
I want to be disguised as a choc-ice.

ARCHITECT. What?

EMPEROR. You must grant my wishes. It's quite easy. You
put a stick between my legs and cover me with a chocolate
coloured breast plate.

ARCHITECT. Your will shall be done.

EMPEROR. Oh! I'm dying, dying! Do as I ask.

(The ARCHITECT brings the stick and the breast plate and
a sack: he disguises the EMPEROR: he arranges the sack
so that the head is showing.)

Oh, mother, dear mother. I am dying.

ARCHITECT. Don't get so excited. You'll get better. Now you're
disguised as a choc-ice.

EMPEROR. Ah .... Ki-----ss .... me.

(They kiss)

EMPEROR. (Panting) I die happy. I leave this mortal world
for .... (His head falls.)

(The ARCHITECT weeps bitterly. He takes the EMPEROR's
hand and kisses it.)

ARCHITECT. (Sobbing) He's dead! He's dead!

(He puts the corpse disguised as a choc-ice in a coffin. He
shuts the coffin.
He begins to dig a grave still crying. Suddenly the coffin
lid opens and the EMPEROR emerges, taking off his disguise.)

EMPEROR. Bastard! Rotten shit-house! You were going to bury
me. You great, four-eyed hermaphroditic nit!

ARCHITECT. Weren't they your orders?

EMPEROR. To put me in the earth? Birdbrain! I'd have woken

up in my grave and then who'd have got me out? With three feet of earth on my belly?

ARCHITECT. Last time ....

EMPEROR. I told you I was to be cremated .... (Sublimely) And you shall scatter my ashes on the waters like those of Byron, Shakespeare, Phoenix, Neptune and Pluto.

ARCHITECT. The other day you got into a temper because I wanted to cremate you and you said you would wake up with your balls half burned off, dancing a jig and shouting Long live the Republic.

EMPEROR. (Very serious) I bend to my slightest whim. Be very careful with death. No mistakes. And this time there was a whole succession of mistakes. Nobody knows how great is my pain!

ARCHITECT. I'm leaving in my canoe.

EMPEROR. (Humbly) Where to?

ARCHITECT. The island opposite. I'm sure it's inhabited.

EMPEROR. What island? I've never seen one around here.

ARCHITECT. That one, over there.

EMPEROR. I can't see anything.

ARCHITECT. The mountain's in the way. I'll move it.

(The ARCHITECT claps his hands.
There is an enormous crash.)

Can you see it now?

EMPEROR. You can move mountains? You can move mountains too? (Sincerely) Don't go. I'll do anything you like. I'll make you Emperor of Assyria. I'll abdicate.

ARCHITECT. I'll go away and find myself a girl.

EMPEROR. Aren't I enough for you?

ARCHITECT. And I'll walk through the towns and strew bottles in the streets so the young people can get drunk and I'll rig

29

up swings so that Grandmas can show their behinds and I'll
buy a zebra and dress it in suede shoes so that it gets
blisters and I'll be very happy because I'll know everybody
and I'll see ....

EMPEROR. Architect, you hate me, admit it.

ARCHITECT. No, I don't hate you.

EMPEROR. I'll make you a present of my dreams, would you
like that?

ARCHITECT. You always dream the same thing - the Garden of
Delights, Bosch. I'm sick of seeing all those women with
roses stuck up their arses.

EMPEROR. You're not an artist! You're just an ignorant peasant!
You know nothing about the sublime, you only like the dress.

ARCHITECT. Which one is better? You never told me anything
about it.

EMPEROR. Run to my Imperial wardrobe and pick any costume
that takes your fancy.

ARCHITECT. When I go away I'll have all the costumes I like.
I'll dress up in matches, in a vague indifinable way. I'll
have tin drawers and electric neckties, coffee-cup jackets
and pearl grey shirts surrounded by an infinite line of
lorries loaded with houses ....

EMPEROR. You poor simpleton, plaything of any illusion.
(Pause) Shall I circumcise you? I'll keep your prepus on an
altar and it will perform miracles like Christ's fifty-six:.

ARCHITECT. Will you teach me philosophy?

EMPEROR. Ah! Philosophy! Philosophy!

(Suddenly going down on all fours.)

I am a sacred elephant. Climb on my back and we'll go
to the sacred year of Brahma.

(The ARCHITECT mounts him.)

Put your chain round my trunk.

(The ARCHITECT does so.)

30

Now make me go forward and pray.

ARCHITECT. Forward, white elephant ....

EMPEROR. I'm a sacred elephant, I'm pink.

ARCHITECT. Forward sacred, pink elephant. We are going on a pilgrimage to see Brahma of the Fourteen hands. We'll get ourselves blessed fourteen times. Long live God!

(The EMPEROR throws him down.)

EMPEROR. What were those blasphemous words you spoke?

ARCHITECT. Long live God!

EMPEROR. Long live God? Ah! Well, I don't know if it's blasphemy. We'd have to read the Summa Theologica or at least an illustrated Bible.

ARCHITECT. Before I go I'd like to tell you something.

EMPEROR. Tell me everything .... I am your father, mother, I am everything to you. (Pause) Just one moment, I'm being called on the red 'phone.

(Ceremoniously he mimes the scene with the telephone.)

Yes, this is the President. (Pause) Hallo! Hallo! How are you Mr. President? (Pause) You're a great guy. Always ready with a joke! (Pretending to redden) A declaration. Mr. President we're not schoolboys any longer. (Pause) Don't take it that way, I didn't know you were a homosexual. You want to make a declaration? To me? Why, you sly old reprobate. (Pause) How's that? A declaration of war on my country? (Angrily) Ten thousand centuries look down on you from the height of these skyscrapers. I will exterminate you as a fly exterminates a wild elephant; my people will invade your people and turn them into .... What did you say? A hydrogen bomb will explode over our heads in thirty seconds? Mummy, mummy. (To his secretary) An umbrella.

(The ARCHITECT opens an umbrella and both take cover under it.)

(At the telephone) You ignorant bum! War criminal! You'd kill your own mother-in-law! (To the ARCHITECT) And to think we were all ready to send our bombs in a surprise

31

attack at 5 tomorrow morning. My kingdom for a Phoenix!

(They mime the sound of bombs falling: they die, air-raid victims: they fall into the brushwood: they soon emerge imitating two monkeys: they scratch their heads.)

ARCHITECT. (She-monkey) Mm. Mm. There's not a single man left alive after the atomic deflagration.

EMPEROR. (He-monkey) Mm. Mm! Father Darwin.

(The TWO MONKEYS kiss passionately.)

ARCHITECT. (She-monkey) We'll have to start all over again.

(They hide in a suitable spot a little apart.)

EMPEROR. (Changing tone, very angry) I forbid you to leave, I forbid you to tell me what you were going to, I am in command here and I order you to destroy your canoe.

ARCHITECT. I'll do it now.

EMPEROR. What's the hurry? Hot-headed youth, quick-silver. Tell me. Aren't you happy with me?

ARCHITECT. What does happy mean? You never taught me?

EMPEROR. Happy .... Happy means .... (Angry) Oh fuck, I don't know. (Tenderly) Have you been today?

ARCHITECT. Yes.

EMPEROR. What was it like, hard or soft?

ARCHITECT. Well ....

EMPEROR. Don't you know? Why didn't you tell me you were going. You know how much I like to watch you.

ARCHITECT. It was pretty soft and it smelled like ....

EMPEROR. Never mind the smell. (Calmer) I'm still constipated. (Pause) Things would have been so very different if you had your G.C.E. or if you'd been to a University - or anything. We just don't understand each other. We belong to completely different worlds.

ARCHITECT. I .... (Sincerely) I love you.

EMPEROR. (Almost moved to tears) You're making fun of me.

ARCHITECT. No.

EMPEROR. (Blows his nose: turns full circle and says in a new tone of voice, very emphatic) You have no idea -- Every morning my waking up was shown on Assyrian television. My people watched with such devotion that women wept and men murmured my name. Three hundred naked women, all mute, would run in and tend my delicate body, scenting it with the essence of roses . . . .

ARCHITECT. Tell me what the world is like.

EMPEROR. You mean the civilised world. Wonderful. For ages man has been storing up knowledge, enriching his mind until he attained that miraculous perfection that life is today. Joy, happiness, peace, laughter, understanding every-where. Everything is designed to make man's life easier, his happiness greater, his peace longer-lasting. Man has discovered everything he needs for his well-being and today he is the happiest, the most serene being in all creation. A cup of water!

ARCHITECT. (Talking to a bird the audience cannot see) Bird, bring me a cup of water!

(Short wait. The ARCHITECT sees it take wing and return: he puts out his hand and takes the cup which the bird gives him:)

Thank you.

EMPEROR. (After drinking) Are you talking to birds in their own language now?

ARCHITECT. That's nothing. What's important is what I think. Between you and me there's such a thing as the transmission of thought.

EMPEROR. (Scared) Tell me, seriously can you read my thoughts? What do you see?

ARCHITECT. I want to write. Teach me to be a writer. You must have been a great author.

EMPEROR. (Flattered) I wrote some splendid sonnets. And such plays - with soliloquies and asides. The best writers copied

33

me: Beethoven, D'Annunzio, James Joyce, Charles V, Shakespeare himself and his nephew Terence Rattigan.

ARCHITECT. Tell me how you killed her.

EMPEROR. Who?

ARCHITECT. Well ....

EMPEROR. When? How? When did I tell you about that?

ARCHITECT. Don't you remember?

EMPEROR. Remember? Should I? (Pause) Listen, I am going to go into retreat. I want to spend all my time in meditation. Chain me up.

ARCHITECT. Why do you want to go into retreat now?

EMPEROR. (Religious and solemn) Hear my last words. I am tired of life; it is my desire to leave behind all that binds me to the world. I do not wish to be near you. Please don't speak to me again. I shall be alone, lost in meditation.

ARCHITECT. Is this a new game?

EMPEROR. No, it's the truth. Besides I've got to get used to your going away in your canoe.

ARCHITECT. I won't go.

EMPEROR. No more talk. The chain.

(The ARCHITECT brings the chain. The EMPEROR puts the chain round his ankle: he ties himself to a tree.)

ARCHITECT. Where are you going?

EMPEROR. Into my cabin. Never speak to me again.

ARCHITECT. But ....

(The EMPEROR goes into the cabin.)

EMPEROR. (Solemnly) Farewell!

(The EMPEROR disappears inside the cabin.)

34

ARCHITECT. All right, I know it's only a game. Come out.

(Silence.
One by one the EMPEROR's clothes appear through the
skylight.)

But .... what are you undressing for? You'll catch a
chill.

(He looks through the skylight.
The EMPEROR shuts it from the inside.)

Listen, at least let me see you. Open the skylight!

(Silence.
The ARCHITECT listens at the door.)

Are you praying? Open up. Do you hear me? Stop this mumbling. Are you really praying? Do you want to die? I'll tell
you my dream. Listen, I dreamed I was a Sabine woman and
I was living in a very old town. One day soldiers came, led
by Casanova and Don Juan Tenorio and carried me off.
Interested?

(He looks all round: he gestures towards the brushwood.)

Snake! Bring me a sucking pig.

(He soon goes into the brushwood and comes out with the leg
of a sucking pig.)

Emperor of Assyria, your female admirers have just
brought you a sucking pig. Smell it.

(He waves it about.)

But it's your favourite, why don't you come out and get it?

(Silence.
The ARCHITECT leaves the stage and comes back dressed
as a woman: this is a very perfunctory costume and can be
easily put on and taken off.)

Look through the crack, look at the pretty girl who's just
landed on the island.

(The ARCHITECT minces up and down.)

ARCHITECT. (Woman) Emperor, come out. I am your humble
    slave. I make you a present of the finest liqueurs, the most
    succulent dishes, my statuesque body belongs to you.

(Silence)

Architect, what must I do to make the man of my dreams
come out and examine me?

ARCHITECT. You are my woman, you should know better than I.
    In any case he's so jealous I hardly dare stand too close.

ARCHITECT. (Woman) Emperor. Come out a minute. Let my
    lips touch your divine mouth, let my hands caress your ebony
    body, let our bellies join in an eternal union.

ARCHITECT. How beautiful you are! You are so like the Emperor's
    mother, I can't understand why he doesn't surrender to your
    charms.

ARCHITECT. (Woman) Oh Emperor, cruel as the hyenas of the
    desert, if you abandon me like this I must go away with the
    Architect.

ARCHITECT. Don't kiss me so passionately. The Emperor is as
    jealous as a tiger.

ARCHITECT. (Woman) Handsome young man, I close my eyes,
    and when I take   you in my arms I think it is the Emperor.
    How young you are, how attractive. How right the proverb
    is: Like Emperor, like slave. Let me kiss your burning
    belly.

ARCHITECT. Oh! No more. I can't resist. How bewitching you
    are, how beautiful. Even if the Emperor comes out and
    kills me in a fit of jealousy I must surrender to your charms.

(Sounds of kisses. Passionate murmurs. Suddenly the
ARCHITECT goes to the skylight, furious.)

I'm not speaking to you any more. Don't come back and say
you want to be friends. I never want to see you again. I'm
going to get my canoe. I'm going for good. I won't even say
goodbye to you. In a few minutes I shall be sailing for the
island opposite.

(He goes out resolute and angry.
Long silence.

The EMPEROR can be heard murmuring prayers: they
increase in volume.
The door opens: the EMPEROR appears naked or dressed
only in tiny briefs.)

EMPEROR. (Meditating) And I shall build myself a wooden cage
and I shall shut myself inside it. And from there I shall
forgive mankind for the hate it has always shown me. And
I shall forgive my father and my mother the day their under-
bellies met to give me life. I shall forgive my city, my
friends, my nearest and dearest for never having recognised
my worth, for never knowing who I am and I shall forgive,
I shall forgive . . . .

(He looks anxiously first on one side then on the other.
While he is speaking he makes a scarecrow which he puts
on the throne.)

Ah! Chained! Alone at last! No one to contradict me, to
make fun of me, no one to see my weaknesses. Chained!
Bliss! "Vivan las cadenas". My universe: a circle whose
radius is the length of this chain.

(He measures it.)

Let's say, three yards.

(Measures it again.)

Let's say two and a half yards, or perhaps it's three and
a half. So if the radius is three yards, say four, I don't
want to cheat, the area will be R squared, that is 3.1416,
R equals three to the power of nine multiplied by
that makes twelve square yards. What more could the
Housing Authorities ask?

(He snivels: uses his handkerchief.
He begins to dress the scarecrow in the EMPEROR's
clothes, still continuing his monologue.
He tries to climb a tree unsuccessfully.
He jumps in the air trying to see into the distance.
Finally he shouts:)

EMPEROR. Architect! Architect! Come back. Don't leave me
alone. I don't like it. Architect. Arch . . . . (He gets a
grip on himself) I must get organised. No slackness. Rise
at 9 a.m. Quick wash. Meditation. Think on squaring the
circle, write a few sonnets perhaps. And the morning will

be gone before you know it. Lunch at one. Ablutions then a short siesta, wank once, once only but properly, lasting three quarters of an hour, what a pity I haven't got that book. Never mind I'll think about that actress, what's her name, it's on the tip of my tongue, the one with the funny bow legs, very sexy, and the beautiful blonde hair and the bulging belly .... Whoa! After the Siesta ....

(He arranges the scarecrow with careful attention to detail so that it looks just like himself.)

Now you've started talking to yourself; you're becoming schizophrenic. You can't do that. Your balance.

(Pause)

In the afternoon, one hour's remembrance for my family, another for the Architect, or half an hour, no he only deserves a quarter. Dinner Ablutions. Finally bed at....... say ten o'clock. Three or four hours to go to sleep and then it's tomorrow. I shall be able to save: no cinemas, no papers, no Coca-Cola.

(As he speaks he takes off his chain. He looks round and calls sadly:)

Architect! Architect! Come back!

(Imitating the ARCHITECT's voice)

Escalator! Escalator! Escalator!

(Humbly to the scarecrow)

Don't grumble at me, I know that you've been teaching me to talk for a year and I still can't pronounce my 's' properly.

(He bows very low.)

Tell me Emperor about how you wake up in Assyria to the sound of music played by a legion of flautists. Television broadcasts your levee doesn't it? And a hundred thousand slaves marked with your seal and chained, hurried to wash every cell of your divine body with syrups from Afghanistan.

(He pretends to listen to what the EMPEROR is saying.)

38

Oh! No! My life is completely unimportant.

(Pause)

No. I'm not trying to make you beg and pray. My life is
really quite un-interesting.

(Pause)

Where was I? My profession? Quite unimportant.

(Ashamed:) Well, towards the end I had a good salary. How
happy my wife was when they gave me a raise. If I'd gone
on that way I could have used the main lift and had a
key to the Director's washroom.

(Pause.
He goes out: he comes back with a grass skirt and puts it
on ceremoniously, while he continues speaking.)

Who told you? It doesn't really matter: she wasn't quite
herself that day, she'd gone off her head, not right off, but
a little deranged and when I saw her with another man I
didn't say anything to her. The poor thing was crying and
saying to this man, "No, I don't want to". And they were
both naked and so he slipped over onto her and said: "Now,
in front of your husband." And she cried even more and
said "No" and she scratched him and it wasn't 'til later
when he began to move that she got that funny expression in
her eyes; you couldn't see the pupils any more; she suddenly
sighed several times and kissed him on the shoulder and he
was laughing and when they'd finished she started crying
again. And she kept saying she was going, she was going,
but she didn't go, she stayed there under him and they were
both naked and he was laughing and he did it again several
times.

(Pause)

No, no, only three times, I think.

(Pause)

Yes, of course and then he left and he said: "Here's your
wife." And I went and comforted her and stroked her back
and she gave a cry that almost . . . .

(He sits cross-legged on the ground.

39

He weeps)

But we loved each other, she was very good to me, as soon as I showed the least sign of a cold, she would start dosing me up.

(Pause)

My bosses liked me and one day they even said they'd make me a . . . .

(Pause.
He weeps)

My mother?

(Pause)

Sometimes we'd spend the whole afternoon bickering.

(Pause)

She didn't love me the way she did when I was a child. She hated me to death. No, my wife, she really loved me.

(Pause)

Friends . . . . yes, I had friends but . . . . of course they envied me. You've no idea how jealous they were!

(He tries to climb a tree unduccessfully. He jumps up to try and see into the distance.
Finally he shouts:)

Architect! Architect! Come back. Don't leave me alone. Don't leave me alone. I don't like it. Architect. Archi -- I ought to call him Archie . . . . it's nicer.

(He pulls himself together.)

Of course, in the end, I didn't see my friends any more. I had a lot of work and I couldn't keep up with them. When you slave away eight hours a day and take the train and the tube and . . . . I hadn't time for anything and then I was indispensable, or so my bosses told me.

(Pause)

40

When I was small it was different. What dreams I had!
Once, I had a girl-friend and I began to fly, but she didn't
believe me and I knew that one day I'd be Emperor . . . .
like you . . . . Emperor of Assyria, that's what I thought
I'd be. Who could have said that I'd meet you? I dreamed I
was going to be best at everything. That I'd write and be a
great poet - and believe me, if I'd had the time, if I
hadn't had to work all day, I'd have been quite a poet   I'd
have written a book like the "Dunciad" and I'd have had my
own back on all my enemies who were so jealous of me.
They'd have all gone through it! (A sly little laugh) Emperor,
what would you have me do? I am your inferior. Speak.

(Silence)

You're bored.

(Silence)

I'll do it, straight away. It'll cheer you up, you'll see.

(He goes out and comes back with a chamber pot.
 He lifts his skirt and sits on the pot.
 He strains.)

I can't. I'm constipated.

(A long silence.
 The EMPEROR is still sitting on the pot.
 Another long pause.
 The EMPEROR seems very hurt.
 He gets up and takes the chamber pot out.
 He returns without it.
 The EMPEROR begins to cry.)

I could have been a clockmaker. I would have been free.
I could have earned a lot of money all by myself, at home.
I'd have repaired watches - no boss, no one over me, no
one to take the rise.

(He snivels)

When I was small it was different.

(A little more lively:)

You know something? I almost took a mistress. I'd have
been nice to her. Me and my mistress. She was blonde, very

beautiful .... we were happy .... we met in a park
and we talked a long, long time. And we made a date for
the following day. I spent all night painting a heart pierced
with an arrow for her. A big heart, like the ones you find
in Church. And I used my own blood for the red. I pricked
my finger so many times. It hurt.

(He weeps: he looks into the distance and cries tearfully:)

Architect! Architect!

(He pulls himself together:
 He weeps again.
 He walks up and down the stage looking in all directions.)

Architect!

(Pause)

And I never stopped thinking about her. She was very fair,
very beautiful and when I looked all over her body, I began
to grow scales and it seemed as though I were a great fish
slipping between her legs. I made a really good job of the
heart .... It was a bit round perhaps. And I sketched
in an arrow and wrote my name. While I was drawing I
thought I was flying through the air with her and her whole
body was no more than hand and lips to .... Anyway it
was very pretty: the heart, the arrow, the drops of blood.
It was a symbol. The trouble is that later the blood went
black .... She was so beautiful, so fair, we talked for at
least half an hour in the park .... about nothing in particular, you might have said, about the weather, she asked
me where this street was and that one .... but she
could see that in fact, under all those words we were talking
of our .... love .... I know she loved me and when she
said, "It's not as cold as it was last year" I knew that she
meant, "We'll go away together and we'll eat sea urchins
while I cover your hands and pubis with cameras." And
when I answered, "Yes, this time last year you couldn't
have gone walking in the park" it was as though I were
saying, "You are like all the sea-gulls of the world at
siesta time, you sleep resting on me as a bird slips into a
bottle. I can feel the beating of your heart and the rhythm of
your breathing in every pore and from my heart gushes a
crystalline spring to bathe your white feet".......and I
thought of a lot of other things, that's why I spent the whole
night doing that drawing for her. And as I didn't know her
name I decided to call her Liz. The next day I rushed out for

our date. I'd hardly done a stroke of work at the office. My
bosses thought that very strange. I lived through the whole
day thinking of her. I wondered if I should tell my wife. But
I didn't say anything. When I got to the park ....

(He is almost in tears)

She must have got it wrong, she couldn't have understood
.... I went to the park every day for a week, five hours
every evening .... She must have been run over. It
must have been that ....

(Changing tone)

I'm going to dance for you.

(He does a grotesque dance)

I could have danced like a god. What do you think? Am I
boring you?

(Recites)

"Alas, when shall I see the smoking chimneys
 In my little village, and in what season
 Shall I see the walls of my poor house,
 For me a province and so much more?"
I shouldn't have come down here. When will your Majesty
grant audience?

(He takes off his skirt: he is only dressed in his loin cloth.)

Shall I get dressed?

(He goes out and returns with a pair of black lace women's
 panties.)

They smell nice.

(He smells: puts on the panties.)

And then God and his creatures. Us!

(He inspects himself in the panties.)

Not bad, eh? Emperor .... did you know that I gambled
the existence of God on a pin-table. If I won one game out of
three, God existed. I didn't do it the hard way. I know how

43

to handle those machines .... and it was one that I
knew. I lit up the table in a moment. I play the first game:
670 points and I need 1,000.

(He goes out and comes back with a suspender belt.)

I start the second game. First ball a disaster, it slipped
between my legs. 16 points. A record.

(He puts on the suspender belt and adjusts it round the waist.)

I shoot the second. I felt a sort of inspiration, you might say
divine. All the customers were there, panting with excitement.
I made that machine rock like a negro dancing with a white
girl. It did everything I wanted: 300, 400, 500, 600, 700
points. I couldn't do a thing wrong, bonus, points, extra
ball. Final result? I got ....

(He examines himself. He adjusts the belt better.)

It suits me doesn't it? What do you think of my suspender-
belt? Ah! If the Architect were here we could build Babylon
and its hanging gardens again. 973 points, 973! If I take
away the 16 points for the first ball that makes 957, and all
with a single ball. If I could mark up 1,000 that was it, God
existed. I was impatient, I had God there, right in my hand.
I had irrefutable proof of his existence. Farewell the big
clockmaker, the supreme architect, the great order: God
existed and I was going to prove it quite decisively; my name
would be scattered through the text books on Theology - No
more Councils, elucubrations, bishops and doctors, I was
going to reveal all. My name would be in all the papers.

(He goes out and returns with a pair of black stockings.)

I like black ones best, don't you?

(He slips on the stockings very seductively and fastens
 them.
 A cry of anguish:)

Architect! Architect! Come back! I'll talk to you. I won't
shut myself up in my cabin any more.

(He snivels)

Birds, obey me, go and call him, tell him I'm waiting for
him!

(Angrily:)

Did you hear?

(Changing tone)

Now what was it he said? Clu-cli-clu-cli .... No, that's
not it. Imagine him being able to talk to the birds. He's
quite somebody! And he can move mountains ....
Mountain, forward!

(He watches anxiously to see if anything is happening.)

Nothing, not a murmur. Mountain, I order you to fall into
the sea.

(He watches. Silence.)

That man .... He can make day or night, either.

(He goes out . He returns with a brassiere in black lace: he
puts it on.
He puts two peaches in the cups of the brassiere.)

If my mother could see me now. Where was I? 973 points!
God was at my mercy, you might almost have said, I only
had 27 points to get. I never get less even on my worst
days. I send the ball artistically and it falls right into the
bonus triangle. One point every time you touch them and
with my style of play .... I start shaking the ball and it
comes and goes just as I please. Do you see what that means,
Emperor? Do you see what that means, Majesty?

(Suddenly he shouts:)

Architect! Come here, I'm going to have a baby, don't leave
me alone .... a poor lonely woman ....

(He begins to pray.)

"In this vale of tears" ....

(We cannot hear the rest)

Emperor, my mother hated me, believe me, believe me,
I swear it was her fault, her fault I tell you!

(He goes out)

EMPEROR'S VOICE. I can't find it .... Where has that clod-
hopper hidden it? Heaven knows I've told him often enough.
A place for everything and everything in its place. You
never know where he's left anything. A comb! Ugh! A con-
traceptive on this island! Has birth control reached this far?
I'll put it on. Hey! It's my size.

(Shouts:)

Architect! Where did you put my frock? I bet he's rowing
like a maniac or some degenerate from the Olympic Games.
Ah! Youth! What a lot. Look where he's put it. A pretty
frock like that in the drawers with the butterfly collection.

(Pensively)

What did he mean by that? I'm coming now, Emperor.

(He appears with a frock under his arm.)

EMPEROR. All the customers in the cafe were around me and I
was shaking that machine like a devil. It obeyed me, absolutely: 988, 989, 990, 991, 992, 993 .... I only had to
mark up 1,000 points .... and the ball was still up
there. I couldn't lose: when the ball comes down it automatically gives you ten points. I was delirious. God had
used the humblest of mortals to prove His existence.

(He adjusts his stockings very sexily and his suspender
belt, panties and brassiere. He puts on high heeled shoes.
He walks about for a moment.)

How do they manage to walk in these things?

(He teeters forward)

It's a question of getting used to them, I suppose. Cum
amicis deambulare. I could have been a great Latin scholar.
I'm sure that if I start walking in these heels I'll get used to
them before you can say knife and I'll run the Marathon in
them. Very moving my arrival in Athens .... Was it
Athens? In high heels and suspender belt. "Athenians, we
have won the greatest victory of modern times". Then I'll
sell my memoirs to a Sunday paper. Architect!

(Shouts)

Listen, I'm about to become a mother, I'm going to bring a

child into the world. Come to my side.

(Changing tone)

That bastard with his bloody silly canoe .... What does
he know of life?

(He spreads out his costume so that he can put it on: it is
 a Nun's habit: he slips it on.)

Now listen, you'll never believe this. I was marking up
point after point with that ball: 995, 996, 997, 998, 999 and
right at that moment a drunk banged on the pin-table and
WHAM the whole thing stopped - the game was finished, and
like an idiot the thing showed 999, 999!

(He examines his nun's habit.)

I would have made a marvellous Carmelite. But not without
my shoes, no nothing doing.

(Shouts)

999. Can you imagine, Emperor? What am I to believe? Can
I consider those ten points I would automatically have won
as valid? We'd better not talk about the third game. What a
blow! 999 points.

(He walks examining himself.)

Supposing I performed miracles. Carmelites perform
miracles.

(Quotes)

"And so you think it is miraculous to feed a crowd of people
with two measly sardines and a crust of bread, as Christ
did. Christian capitalism has done much better since then."
Quite a man the man who wrote that! He's one of mine.
Emperor, can you hear me - you're very quiet. It's like
talking to a brick wall. Are you angry with me? Don't you
think I'm a nice Carmelite?

(He throws himself at the Emperor-scarecrow's feet: he
 takes one of its legs and strokes it.)

Emperor I'm in love with you. You're the most handsome,
most attractive man I know. For one word from your lips
....

47

(He rises: walks up and down)

I'll have to have my baby alone.

(Shouts)

Architect, it's near my time.

(Indeed his stomach swells abnormally.)

These Nuns have got some wonderful inventions. With a habit like this you can hardly tell when they're pregnant. Father, I confess that .... I .... indulged in wicked actions.

EMPEROR. (Confessor) Miserable creature! How could you dare commit such terrible sacrilege? Dirty bitch! Wretch!

EMPEROR. (Carmelite) Yes, father, the devil tempted me horribly.

EMPEROR. (Confessor) Who did you do it with, slut?

EMPEROR. (Carmelite) With the little old man who lives alone on the fifth floor.

EMPEROR. (Confessor) Harlot, with this human ragbag you have pierced Christ's flesh with another thorn. How many times did you do it, you blaspheming bitch?

EMPEROR. (Carmelite) How many times do you think.

EMPEROR. (Confessor) That's what I'm asking you, you sinful creature.

EMPEROR. (Carmelite) Once, just once .... he's very old.

EMPEROR. (Confessor) No human penance can redeem your fault. Infidel. Atheist!

EMPEROR. (Carmelite) What shall I do, father, to obtain absolution?

EMPEROR. (Confessor) Blasphemer! Tonight you will come to my room with rods and salts. I will undress you and spend the night whipping you. Your sins are so abominable that I too will have to ask God to pardon you and to that, and I too will undress and you shall beat me, dirty bitch!

48

(Changing tone)

Architect! Come here, come quick, I need you.

(Shouts)

I can feel the final pangs. Where's the stretcher?

(He lies on it.)

EMPEROR. Tell me doctor, will it hurt much?

(Silence)

EMPEROR. (Doctor) Breathe like a dog.

(He pants)

EMPEROR. (Doctor: Angrily) Didn't they teach you painless childbirth? Breathe. Like this. Ah! Ah!

(He pants like a dog but not very well.)

EMPEROR. (Doctor) No, not like that. Like this. Ah! Ah!

(He breathes badly)

EMPEROR. (Expectant mother) Doctor, I never could learn it. Help me. I'm alone .... I've got nobody.

EMPEROR. (Doctor) All you can do is fornicate. That's the only thing you can do without training. Ah! Ah!

(He breathes like a dog: he does it well.)

You see how easy it is.

(He breathes badly.)

Useless creature. To think that you got down on all fours with your lover like an animal on heat and now you can't even bark. Oh, the human race! Christ should have been a dog. He would have been crucified on a gaslamp and then the whole doggified human race could have pissed against the lamp-post. Breathe, bitch. Ah! Ah!

EMPEROR. (Mother) Doctor, help me. Give me your hand.

EMPEROR. (Doctor) Noli me tangere!

EMPEROR. (Mother) I can feel the final pangs. It's coming! I can feel it, I can feel it!

EMPEROR. (Doctor) Ah, here's the head, a good head . . . . the shoulders are coming now. Good shoulders.

(Panting the EMPEROR-MOTHER groans, yells, dribbles.)

Here's the trunk, a good trunk. One last push. Another push.

EMPEROR. (Mother) I can't go on, doctor. Put me to sleep. Drug me.

EMPEROR. (Doctor) Who do you think you are, Thomas de Quincey? Drug you! Push, immediately.

(Rending cries)

Here it is. All of it. A fine specimen of an earthman.

(Mother's voice: it groans, cries and then calms.)

A new racial unit. Here it is. They can't accuse you of not co-operating in the defence of the values of our civilisation. One more.

EMPEROR. (Mother) Is it a boy or a girl?

EMPEROR. (Doctor) What do you think? A girl. We only have girls now. A human race consisting entirely of Lesbians. No more wars, religious evangelism, road accidents. A happy human race. The best of all possible worlds. We'll spend all our money on dill-dolls.

EMPEROR. (Mother) Doctor, let me see it.

EMPEROR. (Doctor) Here she is.

EMPEROR. (Mother) How beautiful she is, what a sweet little thing, what a darling! The dead spit of him. Oh, I'm going to be happy. I'm going to sew the baby clothes myself.

(He props himself up on the stretcher rocks the baby and hums to it.)

The dead spit of him, so pretty, so lovable. His face.

EMPEROR. (Doctor) Who's face?

EMPEROR. (Mother) The cathedral clock's. If the clock laughed she'd laugh just like it. And I'm going to call her Boadicea.

EMPEROR. (Doctor) What profession have you in mind for her?

EMPEROR. (Mother) Kinestherapist, that's the smartest! Her hands will massage the backs, thighs and stomachs of the men on earth. It will be the re-incarnation of Mary Magdalen.

(Short pause.
Addressing the EMPEROR-Scarecrow in another tone of voice.)

Emperor, Emperor ....

(A different tone: a cry of pain)

Architect! Architect! Archie

(To the EMPEROR)

You see what he's like. He hates me. He's leaving me to my own miserable fate. He has left for the islands in search of adventure and God knows what he'll find.

(He goes down on all fours.)

Emperor, I am the sacred camel of the desert, climb on my back and I will show you the most fascinating markets for male and female slaves in the West. Climb on my back, Emperor. Beat with your Imperial riding crop, so that my step may be exact and efficient, so that your divine person may be purified through contact with the trained, young, vigorous bodies of youths and maidens ....

(He straightens up.)

What a roughneck! In a canoe. In this century of civilisation, flying saucers, progress, fancy travelling in a canoe. If Icarus, Leonardo da Vinci or Einstein could see! Why did we invent helicopters ?

(Pause)

999 points .... Without that drunk I could have marked up ten points more, automatically. The game, God. Angels.

Heaven and Hell. The good and the wicked. The holy prepus
and its miracles. The host rising to heaven in a chalice
pulled by gold chains. The Council measuring the size of
angels' wings. Statues of the Virgin Mary weeping blood.
Miraculous streams and swimming pools. The ass, the
cow, the crib . . . .

(Pause: Quoting:)

"All that is atrocious, sickening, stinking, vulgar, can be
summed up in one word: God."

That's by one of mine, too. What a man!

(Pause)

Believe me, Emperor, with all the respect I owe you, with
all the veneration I have for you, that a man like the
Architect, open bracket, Grand Architect of Assyria, close
bracket, can travel in a canoe. I'll bet he didn't even take
out an insurance policy. The world is a sorry place!

(Shouts)

Scarab, go and fetch a golden sceptre for the Emperor
immediately!

(He waits. Nothing comes. He looks round anxiously.)

I've taught them bad habits. They do just as they like. And
how can I use the cat o' nine tails to punish them? Modern
education. Progress. The Society for the Prevention of
Cruelty to Animals. Everything's going to the dogs. One day
flying saucers will land on the earth.

(He mimes their arrival.)

Mr. Martian . . . .

(Aside) Assuming they are Martians . . . .

Welcome to Earth.

EMPEROR. (Martian) Glu-tri-tro-piii.

EMPEROR. (To the EMPEROR -Scarecrow) That's how the
Martians talk.

52

(To the MARTIAN)

What did you say?

EMPEROR. (Martian) Tru-tri-looo-piiiii.

EMPEROR. (To the scarecrow) He's talking to me about systems of education.

EMPEROR. (To the MARTIAN) Yes, I understand. You're quite right. With our systems we're rushing towards disaster.

EMPEROR (Martian) Flu-flu-flu-flu-flu-jiii.

EMPEROR. You want to take me to your planet. (Scared) No, no, please. I want to stay here.

EMPEROR (Martian) Tri-clu-tri-clu-tri ....

EMPEROR. I'm the most amusing earthman you've met. (Blushing) Me? Poor me. But I'm just the same as everyone else.

EMPEROR. (Martian) Plu-plu-griiii.

EMPEROR. You're not going to shut me up in a zoo?

EMPEROR. (Martian) Pl-pli.

EMPEROR. Ah! Thank goodness for that.

EMPEROR. (Martian) Jlu-jlu-gni-gni-poooooo.

EMPEROR. The king's daughter is in love with me? She loves me?

EMPEROR. (Martian) Ki-klo-loooo.

EMPEROR. Oh, I'm sorry, I didn't quite understand. Yes, you're very pretty. A bit .... you know ....

EMPEROR (martian) Gri-gri-treeeee.

EMPEROR. How strange. We look funny and ugly to you. I hope you don't mean me .... you must be talking about the others. People just don't wash these days! It's no good your saying any more. I won't go to your zoo or to your town.

(His voice builds to anger.)

I wish to remain on earth. It's useless your telling me that as far as the things of the mind are concerned we are only at the stage of being able to endure pain. However good life may be on Mars, I am sure, without ever having set foot there, that it can't be as good as the Earth.

EMPEROR. (Martian) Tri-tri-tri-trooooo.

EMPEROR. What? I shall die a terrible death in a war, burned by radiation? Well, now listen to me carefully. I don't know Mars, and what"s more I don't want to, but I'd sooner live on Earth a million times with all our wars and troubles than go to your (Ironic) idyllic planet . . . .

(To the scarecrow: changing tone.)

Just think, every morning he takes it into his head to wash in that freezing cold stream. I say to him, Architect, you'll catch pneumonia, but he couldn't care less, he stays under the jet of water taking his shower even if it stings. He douses himself with this water and then to crown all he wants me to do the same. Gone forty . . . . he can't even count now . . . . He doesn't understand a thing! Gone forty! . . . . Incidentally he never told me his age. How does he know his own age I wonder. How old can he be, 25, 36 . . . . He's such a poet! Could he be my son? Perhaps. My son. I should have had a son. I would have taught him to play chess at three or four, and to play the piano. We'd have gone for walks in the park - a baby always attracts the girls. What fun I would have had.

(He stops and shouts)

Architect! Come back! Stop rowing. It's bad for your lungs. You'll develop asthma.

(To the EMPEROR-scarecrow)

A waste of time talking about asthma to a man like that who takes a shower every morning in the coldest stream in the island - always the same one. I'm not saying that you can't risk a shower in summer, in-doors with the stove alight, about midday when the sun is really hot . . . . but you have to be really careful. He throws himself in like a mad thing. So young and already he's got his funny little ways. And then all this business about cutting his hair once a year when Spring returns. How did he work it out without my help?

(He stops in the middle of the stage and shouts:)

Architect! Come here! We'll be friends. We'll build a house together. We'll raise a palace with mazes, we'll make swimming pools that turtles will come and bathe in, I'll give you a car so that you can explore all my thoughts ....

(Very sad)

And pipes belching smoke whose whirls will change to alarm-clocks. I will dry out the marshes so that a cloud of pink flamingo with crowns of silver-paper may emerge from the mud. I will season the most delicious dishes for you and you shall drink liqueurs distilled with the essence of my dreams .... Architect!

(Shouts)

Architect!

(Half crying)

We'll be happy!

(He hangs his head and stays like it for quite some time. He gets a grip on himself: he says emphatically:)

I can imagine you as Emperor. I can imagine you waking up. Assyrian television will transmit the first flutter of your eyelids in close-up .... in every town and hamlet women will weep when they see you ....

(Changing tone)

No, he can't be more than 35, I give him 35 at most. He's such a child, such a poet, of such great spirituality. Fancy calling him Architect.

(He has a bright idea.)

Emperor, we can find out his age. We can work it out ....

(He goes to the cabin.)

Here's his sack -

(The audience cannot see what he is doing: he comes out.)

I'll explain. You'll soon see how easy it is. He cuts his hair once a year and because of some superstition and evil spirits or what have you, he wraps the cuttings in a big leaf and puts them in a sack. So if I count the number of leaves I'll know his age. Do you see Emperor? What brilliant ideas I have. My mother always used to say: how intelligent my son is.

(He goes into the cabin)

EMPEROR'S VOICE. 1, 2, 3 .... There are a lot of leaves
....

(Anxiously)

4, 5, 6, 7 ....

(He stops. Long silence. He comes out frightened.)

I don't believe it, there are hundreds of leaves ....
Could that stream by any chance .... Hundreds of leaves,
a thousand at least .... By taking a shower every day
.... Perhaps a thousand.

(He goes into the Cabin
Long wait
He comes out)

And all with hair inside, hair, some half decayed .... the
Fountain of Youth ....

(Very frightened)

But how .... He never told me .... And I certainly
recognised his hair, the same colour, the same tone ....
How is it that ....

(He runs out terrified
Silence
Enter the ARCHITECT.)

ARCHITECT. (Shouts) Emperor!

(The EMPEROR soon appears, frightened.
They are standing on opposite sides of the stage.)

EMPEROR. Tell me, how old are you?

ARCHITECT. I don't know. Fifteen hundred .... Two thousand
    years. I don't know exactly.

    (The Curtain slowly falls.)

ACT TWO

Scene One

(Same decor.
The ARCHITECT enters, carefully making no noise
He goes to the cabin)

ARCHITECT. (Very softly) Emperor? Are you sleeping?

(He comes out of the cabin and leaves the stage right.
Pause
Stage right a large table appears. The ARCHITECT pushes
it into the centre of the stage.
He gets out a large table cloth and covers the table with it.
He lays a big plate and a huge knife and fork.
He finally sits at table
He ties his serviette
He mimes putting down an enormous creature which is
lying on the table.
He pretends to eat a slice
He finally tidies everything away into the drawer
He turns the cloth inside out: it becomes the cloth of a
Judge's table
From the table drawer he takes masks a bell, and a big
book with gilded edges
He puts on a sort of wig and a Judge's mask.
He rings the bell)

EMPEROR'S VOICE. Architect, what's going on?

(He comes out of the cabin)

ARCHITECT. The accused will step forward and say: "I swear
to tell the truth, the whole truth and nothing but the truth."

EMPEROR. (Raising his right hand) I swear. (In another tone)
Did you get me up at this time just for that?

ARCHITECT. (Raising his mask a moment) I won't tolerate asides, you hear? (He slams back his mask.) The accused may sit if he wishes. And try to be precise in your testimony. We are here to help the cause of justice and to shed some light on your life and the crime of which you are accused.

EMPEROR. What crime?

ARCHITECT. Is the accused married?

EMPEROR. Yes, my lord.

ARCHITECT. How long have you been married?

EMPEROR. I don't know .... ten years ....

ARCHITECT. Remember that all your testimony may be used against you.

EMPEROR. But .... you accuse me .... I mean .... you refer .... to my mother ....

ARCHITECT. The court will ask the questions.

EMPEROR. My mother disappeared.

ARCHITECT. We haven't got to that yet.

EMPEROR. Is it my fault if my mother went off God knows where?

ARCHITECT. We will take into account any extenuating circumstances you may present in your defence.

EMPEROR. This is the end. (In another tone) Architect, stop this game. I'm really hurt by the way you talk to me. Do you understand? (Very tenderly) I can talk with my feet the way you taught me. Look.

(He lies down on the ground, feet in the air and starts to wiggle them.)

ARCHITECT. (Taking off his mask and wig) You're starting that filth again.

(The EMPEROR wiggles his feet again)

Always the same thing.

EMPEROR. Did you understand?

59

ARCHITECT. Everything. But you don't understand anything.

EMPEROR. I understand everything.

> (The ARCHITECT lies down behind the table.
> Nothing is visible except his wiggling feet.)

ARCHITECT. I'll bet you can't understand what I am saying.

> (The EMPEROR laughs.)

EMPEROR. Not so fast. You'll see that I can read everything.
"Here my imagination lacks power to keep the memory of
such a great sight."

> (The ARCHITECT continues to wiggle his feet.
> The EMPEROR translates.)

"And just as two wheels obey the same action so my heart
and mind being of one accord are transported elsewhere by
the sacred love which moves the sun and the stars."

> (The ARCHITECT reappears, furious.
> He puts on his mask and his wig again.)

ARCHITECT. The court will discover everything. The first
witness we are going to call is your own wife.

EMPEROR. Please, leave her out of this. She doesn't know anything. She won't be able to tell you anything.

ARCHITECT. Silence. Bring in the first witness.

> (The EMPEROR disguises himself as a "Wife": he puts on
> a mask)

ARCHITECT. Are you the wife of the accused?

EMPEROR. (Wife) Yes, my lord.

ARCHITECT. Do you love each other?

EMPEROR. (Wife) Well, you know, we'd been married a long
time.

ARCHITECT. Did you love him?

EMPEROR. (Wife) I saw so little of him. He went out in the morning early and came home late at night. Recently we haven't spoken to each other at all.

ARCHITECT. Has it always been like this?

EMPEROR. (Wife) Oh, no, at the beginning he was like a madman. He said he could fly. He never stopped talking. He dreamed he would be Emperor.

ARCHITECT. And later?

EMPEROR. (Wife) He even stopped beating me.

ARCHITECT. There was a time when he beat you?

EMPEROR. (Wife) Yes. To show his virility. To get his own back for the countless humiliations he suffered. Afterwards he just didn't have time for it, he came back so tired from the office.

ARCHITECT. What are your feelings towards him?

EMPEROR. (Wife) Well it was never what you might call a wild passionate love affair. I put up with him.

ARCHITECT. Was he aware of this?

EMPEROR. (Wife) Well, although he'll never exactly set the Thames on fire and got carried away by his enthusiasm and made some terrible mistakes, I don't think he harboured any illusions about me.

ARCHITECT. Did you deceive him with other men.

EMPEROR. (Wife) What do you expect me to do all by myself all day. Wait for him?

ARCHITECT. Did you have any children?

EMPEROR. (Wife) No.

ARCHITECT. Was this deliberate?

EMPEROR. (Wife) We just forgot.

ARCHITECT. And what would you say was your secret desire.?

EMPEROR. (Wife) To play the lute in period costume while a knight something like Machiavelli caressed me, and perhaps

61

kissed my naked back through a gap in my bodice. I'd have
liked to have had - although I'm not in any way inclined to
inversion - a harem of women to look after me. I'd have
liked to have had educated chickens and butterflies I could
have carried about with a ribbon and I don't know, a million
things. I think I would have developed a taste for surgery
too. I can see myself operating, dressed all in white with a
big bay window behind me.

(Short pause)

Anyway, he only loved his mother.

ARCHITECT. "He"?

EMPEROR. (Wife) My husband. Can I tell you something.

ARCHITECT. By all means. The Court is here to listen.

(The EMPEROR (Wife) looks all round to make sure that
no one is listening.)

EMPEROR. (Wife) I'm sure he married me to spite his mother.

ARCHITECT. Did he hate her?

EMPEROR. (Wife) He hated her to death and loved her like an
angel. He only lived for her. Do you think it was normal
for a man of his age to be tied to her apron strings day and
night? He didn't need a wife, he needed a mother. When he
hated her he would do anything to be disagreable to her, even
get married. I was the victim of his revenge.

(The EMPEROR takes off the wife's mask.)

EMPEROR. You've gone out of your mind. You've gone mad.

ARCHITECT. (Takes off his Judge's mask) What's going on?

EMPEROR. You're as mad as he is.

ARCHITECT. You frighten me.

EMPEROR. I do?

ARCHITECT. Who is?

EMPEROR. What do you mean, who is?

62

ARCHITECT. Who's as mad as I am?

EMPEROR. God.

ARCHITECT. Ah!

EMPEROR. Before or after?

EMPEROR. Before or after when?

ARCHITECT. Before what?

EMPEROR. I'm asking if He went made before or after the
creation?

ARCHITECT. Poor chap!

EMPEROR. Do you think He's at the centre of the Earth?

ARCHITECT. Haven't we ever been to see?

EMPEROR. I'm sure that's where He is, right at the geometric
centre, looking at all the women's panties.

ARCHITECT. We've never been to see.

EMPEROR. Let's go and make sure. Ah! I can imagine Him
quietly at the centre, surrounded on all sides by earth,
like a worm, happy and completely dotty, thinking He's
a transistor.

ARCHITECT. Shall I raise the earth?

EMPEROR. Yes, yes.

> (The ARCHITECT raises a piece of earth as though it were
> a trap.
> They both look inside. They get down on the ground to get
> a better look.)

I'll get the binoculars.

> (He returns with the binoculars.
> They watch with great curiosity whatever they can see near
> the Centre of the Earth.)

You can't see a thing. It's pretty damn dark.

(The ARCHITECT nods his agreement and prepares to
shut the earth.)

EMPEROR. (Suddenly very worried) Listen, you're sure no one
can see us?

ARCHITECT. Yes, of course I'm sure.

EMPEROR. Do you think the cabin is well camouflaged?

ARCHITECT. I'm sure it is.

EMPEROR. Don't forget spy-satellites, aeroplanes with photo-
electric cameras, radar, radies-thesists ....

ARCHITECT. Don't worry, no one will find us here.

EMPEROR. And the fire and the smoke. Did you put it right out
so that there's no smoke.

ARCHITECT. Well, there's an occasional puff of smoke.

EMPEROR. You fool, they'll find us, they'll find us.

ARCHITECT. Not a chance.

EMPEROR. We'll be found thanks to you and your negligence.
Who asked you to eat hot food? You're nothing but a Babylonian sybarite. Haven't you ever heard of Sodom and
Gomorrah? You deserve God to raze this island as he razed
those vice-ridden cities. Eating hot food, making smoke. You
know nothing of the hygienic properties of cold meat. Hot-
plate, nettle boiler, egg-sucker, fly-catcher. Let my
Achilles anger fall on you.

ARCHITECT. All right, all right.

(On his knees)

Tell me, do you love me?

(The ARCHITECT goes quickly to the table.
He puts his Judge's mask on again.)

Bring in the second witness. The brother of the accused.

(The EMPEROR puts on the "Brother's" mask.)

64

EMPEROR. (Brother) I know, I must swear to tell the truth . . . .
of course . . . . You know in my profession we have a
great respect for the law, don't you? My brother, the poet.

ARCHITECT. There is a note of irony in your remarks.

EMPEROR. (Brother) Irony? If he were a poet we'd all know.
After all it's a public profession, isn't it. We'd have seen
him on the telly. Anyway, that's what I think. The poet.
Always up in the clouds. Your Highness - sorry - your
Excellency, do you know how he amused himself when he was
a child?

ARCHITECT. Tell us, we are here that everything may be brought
to light.

EMPEROR. (Brother) I must ask the ladies' pardon, but I have
to tell you that my brother had a particular talent which he
used to exercise right there in school: he used to drink his
class-mates urine.

ARCHITECT. Although this information may be of a serious
nature, don't you think . . . .

EMPEROR. (Brother) Pardon me for interrupting you. If that
isn't serious what will you say about what he tried to do
with me? I'll explain.

(The EMPEROR rips off his mask in a fury.)

EMPEROR. No, not that. Leave my brother out of this. I
forbid you. My brother is an idiot. He understands nothing.
You're not to make him speak, send him away. You're
doing the dirty on me. Anyway, I'm not playing any more.
This trial is over.

(He sits on the ground twitching with rage.)

ARCHITECT. (Ringing his bell) No more of this childishness.
Proceed. I will not tolerate any interruptions.

(The EMPEROR stops twitching and gets up very dignified.)

EMPEROR. (Like Cicero in a solemn manner) Quosque tandem
abuteris Catilina, patientia nostra? O patientia mea . . . .
How long, Catilina will you abuse our patience? Rome, our
country . . . .

(Stops and adopts a more familiar tone.)

You're a bastard. You can do anything except question my
brother. My brother is an aquatic animal, closely related to
the cayman, the shark and the hippopotamus. I can imagine
him in the green regions still unknown to man, swimming
half submerged, seeking his prey. And me like an exterm-
inating angel watching his movements. Look at his face and
at mine.

(He stops)

Architect, we will make Assyria a most advanced country,
in our own stamp and image. Under-developed countries
will live free from misery.

ARCHITECT. (Taking off his mask) Emperor, I think . . . .

EMPEROR. Be quiet, dog! Listen to the wind of the centuries
proclaiming our work shall never die.

(Silence)

From the height of these . . . .

(He hesitates)

You will be the architect, the Grand Architect, chief organ-
iser, a pocket god so to speak. Opposite you, supporting
you, the great Emperor, modestly, myself that is, ruling
the destiny of Assyria, leading mankind towards a tomorrow
that sings.

ARCHITECT. I feel as though a huge eye . . . .

EMPEROR. So do I . . . . a huge female eye . . . .

ARCHITECT. It's watching us.

EMPEROR. Yes it is.

ARCHITECT. Why?

EMPEROR. Look at it.

(They look at the sky.)

It's watching our present. Look how long and curved its

66

lashes are.

(With considerable violence)

Cruel Desdemona, cruel as the hyenas in the desert, depart from us.

(They look in desperation.
 To the ARCHITECT:)

It hasn't moved.

(The ARCHITECT grabs the bell violently and seizes his mask
 The EMPEROR does the same.)

ARCHITECT. Witness, you were saying you were going to tell us the things your brother did with you.

EMPEROR. (Brother) My brother, the poet, although I was only ten years old at the time, used to amuse himself by perverting me, by raping me and making me rape him.

(Ripping off his mask)

They were children's games and of no importance.

ARCHITECT. Silence. The witness will continue his testimony.

EMPEROR. I told you. Do you want me to make you a picture? I'll tell you how it happened.

(Furious without his mask)

That's enough, that's enough.

ARCHITECT. Silence in court. The witness will continue.

EMPEROR. (Brother) He waited 'til mother had gone. We were alone in the house; he half filled the bath with olive oil and the fun began. Then came the funniest of the lot. When it was all over he started to tremble and bang himself against the bath. I remember one day he made a huge gash in his hand and he sprinkled his sex with his own blood while he sang a hymn and wept.

(He takes off his mask; begins to weep and sing:)

67

>
> Dies irae, dies illa
> Farewell to a poor dead sinner
> Dies irae, dies illa
> Balls to God etc . . . .

ARCHITECT. (Taking off his Judge's mask and putting on the Mother's) My son, what are you doing, weeping and blaspheming?

EMPEROR. Dies irae, dies illa . . . .

ARCHITECT. (Mother) You're covered in oil. What have you been doing?

EMPEROR. Dies irae, dies illa, the dead all died of cholera!

ARCHITECT. (Mother) Son, it's me, mummy, don't you recognise me? You're only a child, how can you think about death? What's happening? But you're all covered in blood. You've made yourself bleed here. We must call a doctor.

EMPEROR. Mother, I want you to buy me a deep well and for you to plunge me in it and for you to come to see me for a moment every day bringing just enough food to keep me alive.

ARCHITECT. (Mother) My child, what are you saying?

EMPEROR. On Sundays you'll switch the radio on for me so that I can hear the baseball scores. Will you?

ARCHITECT. (Mother) My son, what have you done to make you so sad?

EMPEROR. Mummy, I've perverted him.

ARCHITECT. (Mother) Your brother?

EMPEROR. (Rising: brutally) My Lord. With the consent of those present I wish to conduct my own defense. A great poet once said: "Little bastard, big bastard, we're all bastards." That's the real truth. I wish to know in whose name you judge me?

ARCHITECT. We represent justice.

EMPEROR. Justice? What justice? What is justice? Justice is a certain number of men like you and me who escape this same justice for the most part through hypocrisy and trickery. Condemn someone for attempted murder when he never wished to kill anyone? What's more, I don't want to be like everyone else. I forget good advice. I've forgotten that I was advised to cry to create a good impression, to appear to repent. To hell with all advice. And in any case why all these courtroom tricks? Just so that we can go on playing this great big farce called Justice. If I cry, if I assume a contrite air, you won't be deceived by my tears or my repentance, but you'll know that I'm playing my part in this piece of blood and thunder and you'll take it into consideration when you come to deliver the sentence. You're here to teach me a lesson: but you know that the same lesson can be taught to anyone, to you for a start. Well up you, with your trials, your comic opera judges, your puppet lawyers and your vindictive prisons.

(Suddenly the ARCHITECT takes off his wig and his robe and says:)

ARCHITECT. (Clapping his hands)
I went away with Alice
With Alice I came back
The last one to run out of here'

(Very slowly and getting ready to go)

's a cuckold, beat you back!

(They run out as fast as they can.)

EMPEROR'S VOICE. You're a cheat, you've been practising.

(In the distance can be heard laughter and sounds of falling. Soon the ARCHITECT enters.)

ARCHITECT. I'm waiting for you here eating a dromedary's egg, sprinkled with pheasant sauce. Don't be afraid I'm not going to fight you. He! Toro! Toro!

EMPEROR'S VOICE. Moo! Moo!

ARCHITECT. A fine pair of horns. Even quite respectable people can grow them.

(Enter the EMPEROR with a pair of horns on his head.)

EMPEROR. (Plaintively) To think that once you were like a grandmother to me. You loved me, you couldn't do a thing without me. I taught you everything. Now you've no respect for me. None at all. If my ancestors could see. A pair of horns. A pair of horns that his lordship over there planted on me by witchcraft and for why? Because he beat me to the pine tree in the clearing.

(He moans and weeps)

ARCHITECT. Oh! Golden bull, bronze bull, inheritor of Taurus.

EMPEROR. Are you my sacred cow?

ARCHITECT. I am your cow and your blushing camel.

EMPEROR. Then scratch my leg.

(He stretches out a leg: the ARCHITECT scratches it for a moment.)

No, not like that. Do it better. Underneath.

(The ARCHITECT does it better)

ARCHITECT. I'm tired of scratching you. As soon as I start you go to sleep.

EMPEROR. I go to sleep? Is this how you treat the Emperor of Assyria? An Emperor of Assyria, what's more, with a pair of horns - and that's not nothing. Long live the monarchy.

ARCHITECT. Every night it's the same, "Scratch me a little 'til I go to sleep", and then you begin to snore like a pair of forge bellows. But as soon as I stop scratching, silence, you open one eye and you say, "Go on scratching, I'm not asleep yet."

EMPEROR. Take away my horns. Don't forget I've got my dignity to consider. Besides they're heavy and I can't move my head properly.

ARCHITECT. How would you like them to disappear? Shall I clap my hands once?

EMPEROR. Are you mad? Clap your hands. Never! Do you know what I dreamed last night? .... I was being whipped and I was crying. A young girl in my dream said to me: "Don't cry ...." I answered her: "You can see what terrible pain I am in." She laughed and said: "How can you

be in pain if it's only a dream? You're not in the real
world." I told her she was mistaken. She answered that to
prove she was right I only had to clap my hands. I did and I
found myself with my hands together inside the cabin.
Suddenly, sitting on my bed, wide awake.

ARCHITECT. Yes, I saw you, and heard you.

EMPEROR. Imagine if you clap your hands and .... I wake
up from this dream which I think is real .... to ....
You think you're with me in another world .... Better
the devil you know.

(Suddenly and very ostentatiously he joins his hands as
though he were going to clap them. He hesitates a few
moments.
He is going to clap his hands. Slowly, he stops. Turns his
head to the ARCHITECT.)

When are you going to get rid of these bloody horns, for
Christ's sake?

ARCHITECT. All right, don't get into a state. It's easy really.
Go and rub yourself against the trunk of a coconut palm and
they'll fall off.

(The EMPEROR runs out.)

ARCHITECT. No, not that one. Yes, the other one.

(Pause. Confused noises.
The EMPEROR returns without the horns, still rubbing
his forehead with a leaf.)

EMPEROR. Do I look younger without the horns?

(Furious, the ARCHITECT goes to the table, puts on his
robe and the Judge's mask, saying:)

ARCHITECT. After hearing the accused's brother the court
calls the following witness: Mr. Samson.

(The EMPEROR puts on Mr. Samson's mask.)

EMPEROR. (Samson) I swear to tell the turth.

ARCHITECT. Where did you know the accused?

EMPEROR. (Samson) Playing at the pin-table.

ARCHITECT. You only saw him then?

EMPEROR. (Samson) No, one day he asked me to help him.
Anyway, he asked me to dinner and I accepted.

ARCHITECT. What for?

EMPEROR. (Samson) To be an angel.

ARCHITECT. To be an angel?

EMPEROR. (Samson) Yes, in a church.

ARCHITECT. Kindly tell us about it.

EMPEROR. (Samson) When the church was empty, about 11 in
the evening, we used to slip into the choir, high up. He used
to get undressed and stick a few feathers on his back, ten
or twelve. Then he got into a harness with a lot of ropes
attached and I pushed him out into the air. He used to swing
back and forth, like an angel or an archangel and when he'd
had enough I used to pull him up. He always lost half his
feathers. I wonder what the church staff used to think in
the morning when they found them all over the floor.

ARCHITECT. Did you know his mother?

EMPEROR. (Samson) Yes, the accused said that if I would do it
for him, to his mother, he would give me all the treasures
of the earth.

ARCHITECT. You refused of course.

EMPEROR. (Samson) I'm no criminal thank you. Be an angel,
I don't mind. Once in a while, why not? But from that to
killing .... And then you should have seen them in the
cinema. I caught sight of them one day, quite by chance,
you'd have said a couple of lovers.

ARCHITECT. Thank you for these details. The court wishes to
hear the accused's wife once again.

(The EMPEROR changes mask.)

EMPEROR. (Wife) You still need my testimony?

72

ARCHITECT. The court wishes to know your private convictions on the relationship between the accused and his mother.

EMPEROR. (Wife) I've told you already. Sometimes they loved each other, sometimes they hated each other, depending on the moment.

ARCHITECT. Do you think there was something ambiguous, incestuous, between them?

EMPEROR. (Wife) As far as that's concerned I can be quite categorical. I don't believe a word of it.

ARCHITECT. Have you heard the evidence of the previous witness?

EMPEROR. (Wife) Just stories. My husband was impetuous, spirited by temperament. But he never had incestuous rela--tions with his mother. And here's the proof. Shortly before she disappeared, they were going through a period of the most violent hate. His mother asked for an interview and my husband accepted on condition first, that his mother pay him a considerable sum for every minute of the interview, second that she should masturbate me with her "maternal mouth". He said it was so that she should commit the worst of sins. That's what he told me. He's always been such an innocent.

ARCHITECT. And what does this prove?

EMPEROR. (Wife) This proves that there was never anything ambiguous between them otherwise he wouldn't have made me come and tell you as though it were something exceptional. I've just remembered a detail which may interest the court.

ARCHITECT. Kindly tell us.

EMPEROR. (Wife) Recently, when she visited he asked me to cover his eyes with sticking plaster and cotton. Sometimes he would even speak to her but they would be in different rooms.

(The EMPEROR tears off his mask.)

EMPEROR. I bet you're going to condemn me. Answer!

ARCHITECT. An eye for an eye, a tooth for a tooth.

(Very sadly the EMPEROR walks right round the stage, sits on the ground turning his back to the ARCHITECT and puts his head in his hands.
The ARCHITECT watches him somewhat annoyed. Then seeing that it looks serious, he goes to him. He examines him minutely and finally takes off his mask.)

ARCHITECT. What's the matter with you?

(The EMPEROR shudders weakly.

Come on, calm down, it's not as serious as all that. Do you want a handkerchief?

(The EMPEROR nods.
The ARCHITECT addresses the highest branches of a tree which is invisible to the audience.

Tree, give me one of your leaves.

(And a leaf falls immediately, quite a big one.
The ARCHITECT takes it.)

Here, a handkerchief!

(The EMPEROR uses it and throws the hankerchief-leaf away angrily, then he turns his back on the ARCHITECT.)

Does sir want anything else?

(The EMPEROR moans.)

Yes, I know. It's true. You were the Emperor, you still are the Emperor of Assyria. When you got up in the morning all the trains and sirens screamed to tell the people that you had just woken up.

(After saying these words, he goes to see what is happening.
The EMPEROR still isn't listening.)

Ten thousand Amazons, with statuesque bodies, naked, in your apartments ....

(Suddenly the EMPEROR gets up and fills his lungs as though he were imitating a ham actor.
Total grandiloquence.)

EMPEROR. Ten thousand Amazons, my father imported direct

from the East Indies, would rush naked into my apartment in the morning and kiss my finger-tips while they sang the Imperial song in chorus. The refrain goes like this:
'God keep our Emperor for all eternity
May he be granted immortality. "
Such echoes! Ten thousand . . . .

(Aside)

Even if my room had been a stadium . . . .

(Once more with emphasis)

My life has always borne the mark of a unique destiny in the great universal plan of fat; it was an example for the generations to come, in word for posterity.

(Pause. He sits down.)

You're right, I tried to kill my mother. Samson was telling the truth.

(Suddenly gets up: with strength and conviction.)

And so what? I tried to kill her. So? If you think you're going to give me a complex about it, you're quite wrong. I couldn't care less.

(He is suddenly seized by anxiety again. He crawls on his knees up to the ARCHITECT.)

Tell me, you love me just the same, don't you?

ARCHITECT. You never told me about this attempted crime.

EMPEROR. (Rising: Very dignified) I have my secrets.

ARCHITECT. So I see!

EMPEROR. If you want to know the truth, I only ever loved one creature: my Alsatian. He came to meet me every day. We would go for walks together like two lovers: Pegasus and Paris. I didn't need an alarm. He would run in every morning and lick my hands. Incidentally, that often saved me the trouble of washing them. Thanks to him I stopped confiding in my billiard team. He was very faithful to me, isn't that what they say?

(The ARCHITECT gets down on all fours, puts a lead round
his neck and puts a cowl on his head.)

ARCHITECT. I'm your Alsatian of the Islands.

EMPEROR. Medor. Seek it, boy! Seek it!

(The ARCHITECT begins to scratch the sand like an
Alsatian.)

Let's see what my faithful dog will find.

(The ARCHITECT continues scratching and barks.
He finally takes a live partridge from the ground which he
takes in his jaws and carries out, happy.
He returns.
The EMPEROR strokes him tenderly and pats him on the
back.)

"In the order of creation, only man can inspire sustained
disgust, the repugnance an animal inspires is temporary."

(The dog-ARCHITECT approves happily and barks joyously.)

He was really one of mine. That's it, stay by my side always
like a dog and I will love you for all eternity. Like the dog
Cerberus and Homer together we shall explore the kingdoms
hidden deep on the floor of the Ocean!

(He goes blind and puts on dark glasses.
He takes a stick. The dog guides him.)

EMPEROR. (Blind: solemn voice) "Sing, O my muse, the anger of
Achilles". I think I've said that already. Something for a
poor beggar blind from birth who can't earn his living. A
little something. Thank you, kind lady, God give you life
and preserve your sight for many years. Alms for the love
of God. For the love of God .... You know, now that I'm
blind I've never seen God so clearly. O Lord, now that my
eyes are blind I see you with the eyes of faith. Oh, Lord!
How happy I am. I feel, like Saint Theresa of Avila, that you
have put a sword up my arse.

ARCHITECT. (In dog language) In my bowels.

EMPEROR. In my bowels, that's it. I feel that you have put a
flaming sword in my bowels that gives me heavenly joy and
pain. O Lord, I feel too, like the Saint, that devils are

playing ball with my soul. O Lord, at last I have found faith.
I wish the whole of mankind to be witness to this event. I
want my dog to have faith too. Tell me, dog, do you have
faith in God.

(Incomprehensible barks from the Alsatian-ARCHITECT.)

You saracen apostate, don't you believe in God?

(He is about to beat him, but the dog runs off.
He is reduced to groping to right and to left with his stick
like a blind man.)

Bloody animal. Come to my side. It's the voice of revealed
faith.

(He hits out on all sides, trying to hit the dog who stands
laughing at him.)

I'll start a crusade of blind believers to fight all the atheist
dogs on the earth with bayonettes. Bloody animal. Come
here. Kneel down with me, I'm going to pray.

(He flails about with his cane right and left.
The dog teases him, barks.)

And you're still making fun of me. Rotten little coyote
from the pampas. Poor thing. He'll never understand the
the sovereign virtues of pandarism.

(The ARCHITECT takes off his cowl and returns to the court.)

ARCHITECT. (Judge) Bring in the next witness.

(The EMPEROR takes off his dark glasses, grumbling.)

I said bring in the witness. Mrs. Olympia von Kant.

EMPEROR. (Olympia von Kant) How can I help you?

ARCHITECT. Did you know the accused's mother?

EMPEROR. (Olympia) How could I help it. She was my best
friend. We were childhood companions. We were expelled
from the same school.

ARCHITECT. Why were you expelled?

EMPEROR. (Olympia) For childish pranks. We were always
   playing doctors with no clothes on. We used to take each
   other's temperature, perform all sorts of operations on
   each other, empty inkwells on our heads so that the ink
   ran slowly down to our feet .... Of course, they were so
   old-fashioned in those days you can imagine what they
   thought. Of course, we used to kiss each other, but why
   not? We were two little girls whose life was just beginning.
   However, they expelled us.

ARCHITECT. How old were you?

EMPEROR. (Olympia) She was a little older than I. Just two
   little girls. Pranks, harmless pranks, however, we're not
   here to discuss that I imagine.

ARCHITECT. It is a matter of some interest. How old were you
   when you were expelled?

EMPEROR. (Olympia) Who? Me?

   (Very serious)

   Barely twenty.

ARCHITECT. Oh!

   (Tense silence)

   Of course, you know the accused?

EMPEROR. (Olympia) The love of his mother's life: she only
   lived for him. And I always thought he loved her just as
   passionately.

ARCHITECT. Didn't they ever quarrel?

EMPEROR. (Olympia) A few days before his mother disappeared,
   dis-a-ppeared -

ARCHITECT. What are you trying to suggest by this ironic tone?

EMPEROR. (Olympia) I don't think anybody ever disappears,
   they're got rid of.

ARCHITECT. You realise the gravity of your accusation?

EMPEROR. (Olympia) I'm not interfering. All I'm saying is that

78

a few days before the disappearance an incident occurred which she told me about and which I think is worthwhile telling you. While she was asleep, her son crept up to her without a sound, carefully placed a fork, salt, a napkin and a butcher's knife, near the bed. He very carefully brought the knife to his mother's throat and when he delivered a blow that should have cut her head off she moved aside. It seems that the accused, instead of feeling embarrassed, got the giggles.

(The EMPEROR takes off Olympia's mask and is shaken with hysterical laughter.)

EMPEROR. Best mother's meat! A Model butcher's. This week's star offer.

(He laughs heartily.
Suddenly he turns to the ARCHITECT very serious.
Sadly)

I never told you anything, but, do you know, when I'm away from you ....

(Gaily)

To think I could have given her the chop and parcelled her out in steaks. My mother in tournedos.

(Sad again)

You never knew, but if I leave you to go ....

(Dignified)

And pass a motion it's because ....

(He laughs)

My mother was quite a character! I trust you don't believe a word of what Olympia, Mrs. Olympia von Kant told you?

(Sadly)

Well today you shall know all. I shall tell you the truth. I am leaving you to blaspheme.

ARCHITECT. Why? Can't you blaspheme with me?

EMPEROR. (Sad) Please, I don't want to cause offence. Don't forget those historic words: "If thy right hand offend thee, cut it off." - "If thy foot" ..... Is that why there are so many one-legged people about at this moment?

ARCHITECT. You won't cause offence. If you like, we can both blaspheme right away.

EMPEROR. (Worried) Both of us? You and me? Blaspheme?

ARCHITECT. Yes, it'll be marvellous!

EMPEROR. Why would you say if we blasphemed to music?

ARCHITECT. An excellent idea!

EMPEROR. What's the sort of music most likely to rile God.

ARCHITECT. You should know better than me.

EMPEROR. If we blasphemed to military music. He'd like that about as much as a kick up the arse.

　　(Sad)

Do you know what I do exactly when I go away? I defecate in the most refined manner, in a state of absolute calm. Then, using the end-product as paint, I write: "God is a son of a bitch" .... Do you think He'll change me into a pillar of salt one day?

ARCHITECT. Why is He going to change you into a pillar of salt, now?

EMPEROR. (Grandiloquent) Poor fool. You haven't read the Bible. It's unbelievable. Oh, the youth of today! Didn't you know? God can change you into a pillar of salt as easily as he can send down fire from heaven or flood the Earth in ten seconds flat.

ARCHITECT. All right, are we going to blaspheme together or not?

EMPEROR. Aren't you afraid?

ARCHITECT. But you .... you ....

EMPEROR. Don't remind me of my youthful peccadilloes. You know nothing of the weakness of the flesh. How could you? Listen to me.

(He takes up a pose like a tenor and sings forcefully like an operatic aria.)

Balls to God. Balls to his divine image. Balls to his omnipresence.

(To the ARCHITECT)

Well, you might at least put in tralala-tralala. I hate God and all His miracles.

ARCHITECT. Tralala-tralala.

EMPEROR. Dog! How dare you interrupt me!

ARCHITECT. But you asked me to . . . .

EMPEROR. Shut up! Can't you see I'm following my inspiration? Do you think it's that easy to sing opera?

(Pause)

By the way, where were we in the trial?

ARCHITECT. Are you interested in it now?

EMPEROR. Go back to your place immediately. Shall we never get justice on this damned isle? If Cicero were alive, he'd cook up one or two orations.

(The ARCHITECT puts on his Judge's mask.)

ARCHITECT. Justice shall be done. Bring in the next witness. One moment. The court considers that it has heard all the witnesses. We shall now hear what the accused has to say in his defence. What do you say to the letter we found: "As the bird flies to the shore over the heads of the rowing fishermen . . . . "

EMPEROR. Say no more, I recognise my mother's style.

ARCHITECT. (Mumbling as he reads for his own benefit) Ah! Here's something more interesting. "I have always been like a rock, like a library, like a radiesthesist to my son, to him . . . .

EMPEROR. The same old cry: how much she loves me etc. . . . . . .

ARCHITECT. (Mumbles, then reads) "....... when he was a
child, you had to lie him down on the pavement, cover him
with a blanket, then run up, take it off and say 'My child,
my treasure, you died far from your mother ....' " "

EMPEROR. (Impatient) Games, just harmless games. There's
nothing extraordinary in them.

ARCHITECT. Don't forget that she wrote this letter a few days
before her so-called disappearance.

EMPEROR. What's her disappearance got to do with me?

ARCHITECT. (Reading) "I fear the worst, recently he has become
very strange. He makes a fuss about everything. When we
go to the woods on a clear night we don't dance the jig as
we used. I have the impression he's watching me, that he's
......."

(The EMPEROR runs out.
The ARCHITECT takes off his Judge's costume and puts on
the mother's mask then covers his head with a shawl.
The EMPEROR does a wild dance singing:)

> In the night the stars
> Wear ladies shoes and garters
> In the night the stars
> Call me to the centre of my brain.

(Both dance a sort of jig.)

EMPEROR. (Stops suddenly) I'll throw you to my Alsatian.

ARCHITECT. What did you say, my child?

EMPEROR. I'll kill you and let the dog eat you.

ARCHITECT. (Mother) My son, strange things are happening to
you, my poor darling.

EMPEROR. Mummy, I'm very unhappy.

ARCHITECT. (Mother) My child, I'm here to comfort you.

EMPEROR. Will you comfort me always?

ARCHITECT. Where do you get such ideas. Don't you love me
any more?

EMPEROR. Oh yes! Look. I'm a banana. Peel me and eat me
if you like.

ARCHITECT. (Mother) My child, you're a bit light up top.
You're going mad. You're so much alone. You should go out
more. Go to the cinema occasionally.

EMPEROR. Everybody hates me.

ARCHITECT. (Mother) Come and let me nurse you on my lap.

(The EMPEROR puts his head on the ARCHITECT-mother's
lap.)

Don't weep, son. Poor little thing. People all hate you
because you're better than the rest. They're all jealous.

EMPEROR. Mummy, let me sit at your feet like when I was
little.

ARCHITECT. (Mother) Yes, child.

(The ARCHITECT raises his feet. The EMPEROR, sitting
with his back to his 'mother' rests his neck against the
soles of 'her' feet. A difficult position to take and maintain.)

ARCHITECT. (Mother) (Sings a lullaby)

> My tiny little one
> Prettiest of all
> No devil or bogey-man
> Shall do him harm.

(He hums this song while the EMPEROR goes half off to
sleep.
Suddenly the EMPEROR wakes up in a wild frenzy)

EMPEROR. Let my voice echo through the centuries: It's true,
I killed my mother, all by myself.

(The ARCHITECT rushes and puts on the Judge's costume.)

ARCHITECT. Are you aware of the gravity of your statement?

EMPEROR. It doesn't matter. May all the punishments in
heaven and earth fall on me, may I be devoured by a thous-
and carnivorous plants, may a squadron of giant bees pump
the blood from my veins, may I be hung by the feet in

infinite space millions of light-years from this planet, may Satan's dragons roast me until my buttocks are scarlet drums.

ARCHITECT. How did you kill her?

EMPEROR. I hit her on the head with a hammer while she was asleep.

ARCHITECT. Did she die immediately.

EMPEROR. Straight away. (Dreamily) A strange impression - vapours seemed to come from her gaping head and I thought I saw a lizard crawl from the wound. He got onto the table opposite me, his bulging neck rising and falling rhythmically and he stared at me. When I looked at him more closely I could see that his face was my face. When I went to grab it, it disappeared like a phantasm.

ARCHITECT. But when ....

EMPEROR. Then, I don't know why, I wanted to cry. I felt very unhappy. I kissed my mother and my hands and lips were smeared with blood. I tried to call her but she didn't answer, and I felt sadder and sadder and then unhappy.

(The EMPEROR looks for her)

Mother. It's me. I didn't mean to hurt you. What's the matter. Why don't you move. Look how you're bleeding. Do you want me to do my tricks for you?

(He contorts himself, clumsily performs false pirouettes. Reciting:)

"The March Hare and the Hatter were drinking tea. A Dormouse was sitting between them in a deep sleep, and the others were leaning ...."

(He groans)

.... their elbows on him as though he were a cushion"
.... Mother I didn't mean to hurt you, I just gave you a gentle tap with the hammer .... "and talking over his head. Very uncomfortable for the Dormouse, thought Alice, but I suppose he can't mind." Did you like that mummy darling. Did I recite it nicely? Speak to me.

84

(Pause)

Say something.

(The ARCHITECT bangs on the table.)

ARCHITECT. (Judge) What did you do with the body? How do you explain the fact that it was never seen again?

EMPEROR. Well ....

(He hangs his head shyly.)

It doesn't matter.

ARCHITECT. The court must know everything.

EMPEROR. The Alsatian we had .... the Als .... the Als .... well he ate the body.

ARCHITECT. But you didn't stop him?

EMPEROR. Me .... well .... what was wrong in it? It took him several days. He ate a bit every day .... I put him into the room.

ARCHITECT. Did he eat everything? Bones as well?

EMPEROR. Those he hadn't gnawed I threw into the dustbins at the Medical School.

ARCHITECT. The court will judge your actions ....

EMPEROR. (Patently insincere) As a ship with sails spread, stops at all the ports on its journey, so shall my pain know all the degrees of suffering.

(Sincere)

Architect, condemn me to death, I know I am guilty. I know I deserve it. I can't bear this life of failure another minute. I think I could have been happy in an aquarium, sitting on a chair surrounded by fish and water. Little girls would have come to see me on Sundays. Instead of that .... Architect, tell me you're .... my friend, tell me that despite what's happened you won't throw me out tonight.

ARCHITECT. We are here to judge you.

EMPEROR. Architect, tell me once that you have condemned me.

(Pause)

Listen, I am your Phoenix.

(He imitates the Phoenix)

Climb on my back and I will take you to the paradise of difficult lessons.

ARCHITECT. No more nonsense. You are in a court of law.

EMPEROR. The articles in evidence against me are your round swans during the last period of the full moon.

ARCHITECT. You will be judged with extreme severity.

EMPEROR. May I ask what my punishment will be?

ARCHITECT. Death.

EMPEROR. May I choose the form of death?

ARCHITECT. Speak!

EMPEROR. I want you to kill me with a hammer. Architect, I want you to kill me.

ARCHITECT. I think we can grant your request.

EMPEROR. But most of all . . . .

ARCHITECT. What?

EMPEROR. I don't ask, I demand, this is the last wish of a condemned man . . . .

ARCHITECT. Speak, for goodness sake.

EMPEROR. After my death . . . .

ARCHITECT. (Taking off his wig) Emperor, are you speaking seriously?

EMPEROR. (Gravely) Very seriously.

ARCHITECT. It was just another game: your sentence, your

86

trial .... but you seem to be taking it seriously.
Emperor, you know how much I like you.

EMPEROR. (Moved) You mean it seriously.

ARCHITECT. Yes, most seriously.

EMPEROR. (Changing tone) But today we weren't playing.

ARCHITECT. Today was just like any other day.

EMPEROR. It was different, you found out a lot of things I
didn't want to tell you.

ARCHITECT. Does it matter? Kiss me?

(The ARCHITECT closes his eyes.
The EMPEROR goes to him and kisses him ceremoniously
on the forehead.)

On the forehead?

EMPEROR. I respect you. What do you know about such things?

ARCHITECT. Teach me, the way you taught me everything.

EMPEROR. Today you will kill me. You condemned me to death
and you must execute the sentence.

ARCHITECT. But death is not a game like the others: it's
irreparable.

EMPEROR. I insist. It's my punishment. I was talking about my
last wishes.

ARCHITECT. Speak.

EMPEROR. I want you .... I want .... that is I
want you to eat me .... to eat me. I want you to be you
and me as well. You will eat all of me, Architect, do you
hear?

(Blackout)

Scene Two

(A few hours later.
On the table which previously served for the trial lies the

naked body of the EMPEROR.
The table is laid for a meal.
When the lights come up on the scene the ARCHITECT
appears with a large napkin tied round his neck.
As the play draws to its close the ARCHITECT assumes
the voice, tone, features and expressions of the EMPEROR.
When the lights return, the ARCHITECT is in the process
of cutting off the EMPEROR'S foot with a knife and fork.)

ARCHITECT. Heavens, he has tough ankles.

(He half saws the foot and vainly tries to detach it.
Addressing the dead EMPEROR's head:)

Hey, Emperor, what the hell did you put in the bones of
your feet, I can't cut them off.

(He goes into the cabin and comes out with a rudimentary
saw.
He saws with this improvised tool. The foot is resistant.)

Kill him .... eat him .... And I'm all alone here.
Who's going to take me to Babylon on an elephant's back
now? Who's going to rub my back before I go to sleep. Who's
going to whip me when I want it?

(He goes to the brushwood.)

Moles, go and fetch me an axe. Let's see if I can finally
get this bloody foot off.

(He stretches out his hand.
Nothing happens.)

What's going on? Why don't you obey me? It's me talking to
you. I'm the Architect. I'm not the Emperor. Bring me an
axe.

(He stretches out his hand. He waits impatiently.
After a long wait an axe appears in the brushwood.)

They took their time, the lazy devils. Don't they obey me
any more? We'll soon see. Thunder and lightening strike
immediately.

(Agonised wait.)

What? Not that either? I feel quite funny. I'm very worried.

I took a shower in the Fountain of Youth. I did all the exercises and yet they don't obey me any more.

(Thunder and lightning.)

Ah! Good! Better late than never!

(Axe in hand, he goes to the EMPEROR. He hacks away strongly at the foot and manages to cut it off. He takes the foot in his hands. He examines it closely.)

There are his five toes. His corns. A good foot, a bit big, by God. I bet it's not ticklish any more.

(He tickles the sole of the foot but it is he who laughs.)

Eat it just as it is with no sauce .... A bit of salt will work wonders.

(He salts it. He takes a bit and savours it.)

Mmm, it's not bad. I think I'm going to enjoy this.

(He suddenly stops eating very frightened.)

I hope this isn't a fast-day . Is it Friday? I don't think so. And in any case which is the religion which forbids the eating of meat on a Friday? That bastard Emperor (Oh! Pardon!) didn't tell me. In one of them there's this business about Friday and the .... crusades. You know, I can't remember a thing. In another there are harems. It's all a bit mix-up in my head. If I remember rightly they all forbid masturbation .... unless .... where are those bloody religious books. Anyway, what is my religion. Oh we'd better not go into that.

(Suddenly very worried)

The paper, where's that paper?

(He goes into the cabin and comes out with a piece of paper in his hand.)

"When you eat me I want you to dress up as my mother. And particularly don't forget to put on her big lace-up corsets." Yes, I was forgetting the most important thing.

(He goes to the cabin and returns with a large suitcase marked in big letters "My darling mother's clothes".

89

Opening the case.)

What a smell! Oof! She must have wet herself. She smells
worse than the Emperor. And when he took it into his head
to touch his sex you could smell it a mile off. Obsessed he
was - playing with his, sticking it in the air, looking at
it . . . .

(Suddenly he bursts out laughing.)

And when he hid it between his legs, you'd have said he
hadn't got one. He was just a kid.

(He takes out the corset. He puts it on. He begins to lace
 it up.)

What good are all these laces. Just a minute. Aren't I
talking almost like the Emperor? What's happening to me?
I'm talking to myself too. As he said: I am alone. That
gives me the opportunity to do something Shakesperian.
Bloody corse! Who invented this thing? Why did he tell me
to dress-up as his mother? Well, I suppose I'd better not
interfere; it's his business.

(So as to pull the laces more easily he fixes them to a
 branch: he pulls violently.)

I'm suffocating. How did they get groped with all these
knick-knacks?

(He has finally finished lacing up the corset.
 He wraps himself in a shawl and puts on an extravagant hat.)

I'm a wonderful mother! Poppaea isn't in my class. My
womb is ready to give birth to Nero himself . . . .

(Worried)

Didn't the Emperor say that? Down with the Monarchy. I'm
sick of you and your mother. That's all I'm going to do for
you - eat you dressed up as your mother and then I'm
going to sail to new shores in my canoe. I can hear the call
of the ten thousand trumpets of Jericho under the water.
From my womb a light will be born which will guide me to
a country where I will live crushed by the weight of happiness, where children will run with the queens of Sheba and
old men will rule woman with caressing hands.

(He has dressed up as a mother in rather a perfunctory
manner.
He sits down at table and ceremoniously eats another
slice of the EMPEROR's leg.
He stops chewing and speaks, weeping, the the EMPEROR's
head.)

You know, I miss you very much .... I feel all alone
without you. You were very good company. Promise me
you'll come to life again .... Won't you speak to me?
At least tell me you're my friend.

(He waits for a moment.)

Say something, please. Perform a miracle. The Saints
speak after they're dead, you told me yourself. Perform a
miracle for me. Anything .... I just want to feel your
presence. Look at this glass of water. Change it into whisky.

(He raises the glass.)

Come on, make an effort. It's just a little glass, nothing at
all really. If I'd asked you to cast a bell and to make the
sterile women who were going to ring it, fertile, you'd
have cause for complaint, but just some whisky ....

A tiny effort .... Something even easier: change the
water into white wine.

(He waits: nothing happens.)

Into white wine. It's child's play .... Into half wine, half
water.

(Furious)

All right, I'm not talking to you any more .... I'm not
paying any more attention to you. You can finish dying alone.

(He bites the EMPEROR's foot furiously.
He picks up the glass of water and puts it to his lips to
drink. He throws it away furiously.)

Bastard, shit-house. You changed it into Jeyes' fluid. You're
an old queen and a whorehouse saint. If that's a miracle, my
names's Ellen Terry.

(He eats a great hunk of foot.)

What did he mean by that? Jeyes' fluid. So there is an after-life .... beyond. If I had a three-legged table I could get into contact with him. Anyway, I've got the best bit. When I've eaten his brain and all the nucleic acid in it we'll see what we'll see. With his nucleic acid inside me I can do anything.

(He goes to the cabin and returns with a sculptor's board and a drinking straw.)

May I? First I'm going to suck your nucleic acid. Thanks to which .... Now I understand, ... the Jeyes' fluid was for his mother .... for his mother ....

(He laughs)

Thanks to your nucleic acid I shall be the master of your memory, your dreams .... and your thoughts.

(He taps on the chisel placed behind the EMPEROR's ear. He makes a hole: he sticks the straw in: he sucks out the brain, a substance like yogourt trickles down his cheeks. He licks it.)

Ooh!

(He has finished sucking out the brain.)

I feel another man. All right, now I deserve a little nap. Gorillas of the forest go and fetch me a hammock.

(He waits impatiently.)

What? Do you refuse to obey me?

(He goes up to the brushwood.)

Hey! Gorilla! Yes, you. Go and fetch me a hammock immediately.

(He waits for a while.)

Not only you don't obey me but you run away from me. It's the end.

(He sits down groaning sadly.)

I've lost all my authority.

(Blackout)

Scene Three

(Only the EMPEROR's bones are left on the table.
The ARCHITECT now has the same intonation and the same
habits as the EMPEROR.
When the lights go up the ARCHITECT is sucking the last
of the bones.)

ARCHITECT. Now I can't command the animals any more, I
shall train a goat. When I tell him to sign with his hoof
it'll scribble something, when I tell it to imitate Einstein
it'll put out it's tongue; when I tell it to be a bishop it'll
get down on its knees. Emperor, where are you? How did I
manage to eat you so easily? Dust thou art and to dust thou
shalt return .... And the sun? Does the sun still obey
me? We'll soon find out: let there be night.

(Nothing happens.
Sucks the last bone once more.
Puts it down on the table.)

Now I can say quite truthfully that I have finished.

(The bones stay on the table where they form a sort of
dislocated skeleton.)

I'm talking to myself as though he were here. I must try and
stop.

(He bangs the table with his hand and one of the bones rolls
on the ground.
He gets under the table to pick it up.
He disappears completely from the audience's view.)

ARCHITECT'S VOICE: Where's that bloody bone?

(When he re-appears, it is the EMPEROR who comes out
from under the table, dressed as the ARCHITECT.)

EMPEROR-ARCHITECT. Ah! Here it is. Here's the bloody bone.
I must be careful. I knock things down with the back of my
hand. A goat, yes, an educated goat that will become Prin-
cess of Chaldia or Empress, or a lascivious nun.

(He shoves the table with the bones on it: it disappears stage
right.)

93

Away with these scraps of Imperial love-feasts. Alone at
last. This time there's no mistake, I am going to be happy.
A new life is beginning for me. I have forgotten the last
entirely. Better still, I have forgotten the past so that it
may be always present in my mind and so I shall not fall into
any of my past errors. No snivelling sentimentality. Not a
tear for other people.

(He weeps.
Pulls himself together.)

I said not a tear for other people. Serene. Quiet. Happy.
No complications, no suggestions. I shall study and I
shall discover perpetual motion unaided.

(He puts out one foot and looks in the opposite direction.)

Scratch my leg, tickle me.

(Slowly, his face turned in the opposite direction he slips a
hand towards his leg.
As he touches his knee with his hand he says sensously:)

That's it, there, scratch it properly, slowly, a little lower,
with your nails. Harder. With your nails I said. Harder.
Scratch harder. Harder still. Lower. Harder. Harder.

(He is suddenly in a frenzy.
He grabs the scratching hand with the other and holds it as
though it were lifeless. He looks at it in surprise.)

What orgies I shall have. I shall be all alone, the first, the
only one. The best. I must be quite sure no one can see me.
Hidden day and night. And no fire. No cigarettes. The glow
of a cigarette end can be seen on a radar screen ten thousand
miles around. I must take every precaution. I shall sing
operatic arias.

(He sings:)

Figaro-Figaro-Figaro-Figaro-Figaro . . . .
What a man! And because I am alone the human race won't
envy me, won't persecute me. No one will know the talent,
the sole inhabitant of this planet, I mean this desert island,
has. And now, since there's no one here to hear me . . . .

(Crazy with joy:)

Long live me! Long live me! Long live me! And balls to the

others! Long live me! Long live me! Long live me!

(He dances wildly happy.
At that moment the sound of an aeroplane is heard.
The EMPEROR listens for a moment motionless.
Then, like a threatened, hunted animal, looks for a place
to hide, runs in all directions, digs in the ground, trembles,
starts running again and finally buries his head in the sand.
Explosion. Bright glow of flames.
The EMPEROR, his head half buried in the sand sticks his
fingers in his ears and trembles with fright.

A few moments later the ARCHITECT enters.

He is carrying a large suitcase. He has a certain stilted
elegance in his newly pressed clothes.
He endeavours to maintain his composure.
He touches the EMPEROR with the end of his walking stick
and says:)

ARCHITECT. My dear sir, kindly telephone. I am the only
    survivor from the crash.

EMPEROR. (Horrified) Fi, Fi, Figa, Fiiii.

    (He looks at him for a moment, shattered then runs out as
    fast as he can.)

CURTAIN

THE END

THE GRAND CEREMONIAL

CHARACTERS

CAVANOSA

SIL

LYS

THE LOVER

THE MOTHER

SEVERAL NUDE DOLLS

PROLOGUE

Scene One

(Darkness)

CAVANOSA. Mummy! Mummy!

>(Police sirens.
>The lights come up slowly.
>CAVANOSA is sitting on a park bench.
>It is the early part of the night.
>Enter SIL.
>She too sits on the bench.
>Long silence.)

SIL. Are you waiting for someone, too?

CAV. Mmmm . . . .

SIL. I'm sorry. Seeing you sitting there I wondered if you were waiting for someone.

CAV. (Shyly) No.

>(His shyness is so excessive it is almost a caricature. He rubs his hand over his mouth several times, then over the back of his neck.)

SIL. Weren't you calling you mother?

CAV. My mother? Perhaps.

SIL. Are you waiting for her?

CAV. No.

SIL. Where is she?

CAV. (Violently) What's that got to do with it?
(Gently) I'm sorry, mademoiselle.

(Long silence.
He gathers strength from somewhere after making a
great effort.)

CAV. Are you a lesbian?

SIL. What did you say?

CAV. I'm surprised you should speak to me. It's the first time
a woman has every spoken to me. I wondered if you were a
lesbian.

(Long tense silence.)

SIL. You said women never speak to you. What about your mother?

CAV. I'm an orphan, mademoiselle.

SIL. Then why were you calling her?

CAV. I'm sorry, it's a bit silly I know, but I thought if anyone
sees me they'll imagine someone loves me, "in spite of
everything" -- my mother.

SIL. And I fell for it.

CAV. What of it?

SIL. You wanted to know if I was a lesbian. Well I'll tell you ....

CAV. (Cutting in) I'm not interested!

SIL. You're not interested?

CAV. Well, yes, I suppose so.

SIL. And then you told me it was the first time a woman had
spoken to you. It must be nice for you to talk to me.

CAV. I didn't say I liked it. I said I was surprised.

SIL. All right if you don't like it I'll shut up. To tell the truth I
really should go. The person I was waiting for won't turn
up now, it's too late.

(She looks as though she is going but she stays.
Long silence.)

CAV. (Flat voice) I've just killed my mother.

SIL. <u>You</u> have?

CAV. Didn't you hear what I said?

(She would like to say something but doesn't know what.
Long silence.)

CAV. What does it feel like to be sitting next to a murderer? Do
you want a closer look, Look at me. Well, come on, look!

SIL. Yes, yes, I'm looking at you.

CAV. What do you think?

SIL. What do you want me to say? That it's horrible?

CAV. What's horrible?

SIL. Killing someone.

CAV. So I'm horrible. You admit it.

SIL. Well, yes, I suppose so.

CAV. You see, women don't want to talk to me. Today, you
spoke to me and the first thing you do is insult me.

SIL. I didn't insult you.

CAV. So you approve of people killing their mothers?

SIL. I never said that.

CAV. You insulted me, come on, admit it. You hate me. I'm not
in the least surprised. You know, sometimes I say to myself,
you need a girl-friend .... And I go to church and I look
for the ugliest woman there, someone about 40 or 50. When
I've found her I sit in the place next to her and pretend to be
praying, I try to look like a little saint and when she goes
out I try to rub against her and she always, <u>always</u>, insults
me.

SIL. What a stupid idea. Why go looking for that kind of woman?

You should be interested in girls.

CAV. That's it! I never thought of that. I could go dancing, couldn't I? And invite the prettiest girl to do a waltz? ....

(He rises and waltzes round in front of her in a grotesquely flirtatious manner which accentuates his hump and his limp.)

CAV. Look at me then.

SIL. I am looking at you.

(He sits.)

CAV. Did you like it? Will you dance with me next?

SIL. (After a long silence, with conviction) Yes!

CAV. That's the best thing I ever heard! (He laughs loudly.)

(Long silence.)

CAV. Would you be willing to kiss me?

SIL. Of course!

CAV. Go on then.

(Classic attitude of someone waiting to be kissed. She leans towards him to kiss him. When he is sure that she really means it he moves away.)

CAV. (Violently) Don't touch me!

SIL. You're the one who doesn't want to.

CAV. Why should I let myself be kissed by every whore that comes along.

SIL. You're insulting me. I ought to go.

CAV. I'm not stopping you. Go if you want.

SIL. I feel sorry for you.

CAV. (Beside himself) You feel sorry for me, do you? And who are you to feel sorry for me, eh?

102

SIL. I'm sorry, but you called me . . . .

CAV. Yes I called you a whore! Who but a whore would kiss me?
      Tell the truth.

SIL. I'm not like that.

CAV. Then we'd go to a hotel, wouldn't we? And you'd give it to
      me at a special rate because I was "nice".

SIL. You know it's not true.

CAV. How do I know? I don't know any women. Anyway they tell
      me these days it's difficult to tell the difference between the
      whores and the rest.

SIL. Isn't my word enough for you?

CAV. Why did you want to kiss me then?

SIL. People kiss their brothers.

CAV. Yes, but I'm not your brother, or your fiance, or your
      lover!

SIL. I like your face.

CAV. (Ironically) I'm overwhelmed.

      (Silence)

CAV. What's your name?

SIL. I'm called . . . .

CAV. Don't tell me, it's none of my business. And my name isn't
      any of your business either.

SIL. I'd like to know your name.

CAV. If we were in a crowded place in broad daylight would you
      stay with me?

SIL. Why shouldn't I?

CAV. Why shouldn't you?

SIL. It's the truth.

CAV. And would you kiss me as well?

SIL. Yes, I'd kiss you as well.

CAV. Mademoiselle I want to put a most solemn question to you. Will you be my mistress?

(She is about to reply after a moment's brief reflection.)

CAV. In other words, would you be willing to sleep with me?

(She is about to reply after a moment's brief reflection.)

CAV. Would you sleep with me on this bench?

SIL. You don't give me a chance to answer.

CAV. Wait, I can just imagine it. You laying down on the bench with your skirts up and me on top of you trying to find out how to use my penis.

SIL. Please, that's enough! Be quiet!

CAV. Why should I be quiet? Don't you think it would be a romantic sight? We could invite the children on their way home from school. We'd have a full house every night.

SIL. What will you think of next!

CAV. I want to tell you one thing; my penis is very small.

SIL. Men all have this obsession. They say children measure their penis at school.

CAV. What do you take me for? I've never done a thing like that!

SIL. Then how do you know?

CAV. It's quite obvious! I think it's due to my father being an alchoholic, or perhaps to my mother's having syphilis.

SIL. What good does it do you, saying things like that?

CAV. What harm is there in it?

SIL. Can't you talk of anything besides ....

CAV. Besides .... dirt? Why am I presenting you with this

104

catalogue of horrors, that's it, isn't it?

SIL. If you like.

CAV. Well, then, I'll tell you. I want to dazzle you.

SIL. And is that the way you're going to dazzle me?

CAV. Naturally! For example, once, I remember, I told a woman
that my sex-life consisted entirely of masturbating horses.
I was trying to dazzle her, too. I'm sorry to say I didn't
succeed. I thought she'd say "He's quite different from
other men." I even thought she'd recognise the fact that
my "soul" was unusual, strange, and that the things I'd
told her were not lacking in a certain poetry --- a kind of
black poetry, I think they call it .... But no, she just
looked at me and said, quite matter of fact, "It would be
better if you didn't have these tendencies ...."

SIL. Now I come to think of it you told me you'd never spoken to
a woman.

CAV. And you believed me didn't you?

SIL. So, you tell lies.

CAV. I lie and I don't. To tell you the truth I'm vain enough to
imagine I have a very turbulent "inner life" --- that's what
they call it, isn't it? I imagine I'm having a conversation
with a woman and then I live it. In reality I've never met
the woman I was telling you about. She's just an imaginary
character with whom I exchanged imaginary words.

SIL. You've really never had any kind of relations with women?

CAV. Never.

SIL. You're taking advantage of my ignorance, you're just saying
anything.

CAV. You're getting on my wick, you know that?

SIL. Why take that tone?

CAV. Who are you?

SIL. (Annoyed) And who do you think you are?

CAV. That's it! (Triumphantly) Go on, say it. A poor devil who'd make a cat laugh!

SIL. You're always trying to hurt me.

CAV. Who's the aggressor? You or me?

SIL. The answer to that one is obvious.

CAV. Every night I come to this park. I sit on this bench and I
spend two hours, quietly thinking. And tonight you arrive,
you sit down beside me, you talk to me, you try to kiss me.

SIL. You asked me to.

CAV. I did? I asked you to sit down beside me and talk to me?

SIL. I'm talking about the kiss.

CAV. Don't change the subject.

SIL. That's what you're doing.

CAV. What are you after? You want me to tell you you're in the
right. Well, I won't. I daresay you're quite used to men making
making fools of themselves for a "favour" --- that's the
word isn't it? Well, I'm not like that.

(Long silence.
Police siren.)

SIL. Can I tell you something?

(Long silence.)

SIL. I find you very attractive. I think that any woman would
fall in love with you, in spite of everything.

CAV. What are you insinuating? What do you mean "in spite of
everything"?

SIL. I mean in spite of your strange ways.

CAV. Am I responsible for my body? Did I ask God, that sonof-
abitch (always supposing He exists, which is impossible) to
bring me into the world? Did I choose this body and this
riff-raff?

SIL. I was thinking more of the things you say, your idea.......

106

(Police siren)

SIL. I just can't understand it. You go to church to try and get
near the most unattractive people but when I come to you
and talk to you and treat you in a friendly manner you don't
just reject me, you hurt me and insult me as well.

CAV. Where did you get the idea I go to church on the look out
for whatever it was? I've never set foot inside any place of
worship since the day I was born.

SIL. But you told me yourself.

CAV. And you believed me? What a fool you are!

SIL. That was a lie as well?

CAV. Of course.

SIL. Why did you say it then?

CAV. It's simple really. I thought, what can I say to please her?
And I decided the best thing to do would be to snivel a bit
and confess . . . .

SIL. I didn't see you snivelling.

CAV. Well then, look pitiful. And tell you that lie about looking
for a woman. And you believed me. And if you believed me.
And if you believed me it was because you thought it might
possibly be true. Isn't that right? Answer me!

SIL. If you told me it was so why should I think otherwise?

CAV. Because you should. (He calms down)

SIL. I don't know where I am. How could I know?

CAV. I'll tell you why women don't speak to me. I'm tempted to
admit that it's not only because of my . . . . shall we say,
the way I'm made . . . . but for another reason.

SIL. What's that?

CAV. Can't you guess?

SIL. No.

CAV. They realise the only way I can enjoy them is with a whip. Didn't you notice that?

SIL. No.

CAV. Don't you understand that in the entirely inconceivable, impossible event that we should "love" each other, I could only enjoy you by torturing you?

SIL. I hadn't noticed.

CAV. Excuse me if I ask you a rude question. Have you been in love?

SIL. Yes. Have you forgotten your first question?

CAV. "Are you lesbian"?

SIL. I don't think I am, but I fell in love with my history teacher. She was a woman of about 30 or 40, quite pretty she was.

CAV. Did you sleep with her?

SIL. You always think the worst, don't you? I was just a girl, it was purely platonic. I remember she used to sit on my desk when she was teaching me. Need I say I was her best pupil. That lesson was so intense. Everyone knew. I had created a "history teacher" psychosis. I was always talking about her, imagining her dressed in strange ways. The whole class, probably the whole school knew about it. And of course, she knew as well. And she payed me special attention. One day she was posted somewhere in the provinces .... Then I fell in love with a man. He died and one morning I gathered his ashes in a little box like this. The family ....

CAV. Don't you think you've bored me enough with your silly school-girl stories?

SIL. You were asking me?

CAV. Don't kid yourself.

SIL. I wonder why I put up with the way you treat me.

CAV. Who are you to put up with it or not to put up with it?

SIL. (Violently) And who are you then?

CAV. I'm fed up with your school-girl chatter.

SIL. All right, I'm going.

CAV. Go on then, I'm not keeping you.

SIL. I'm going.

> (Long wait.
> CAVANOSA is quite indifferent. She takes a few steps.
> Suddenly she turns round and says angrily:)

SIL. You're hateful!

> (He laughs, a long laugh.
> SIL goes angrily.
> CANANOSA is alone on stage - he sits on the bench.
> Blackout.)

CAV. Mummy, mummy!

> (Police siren.)

Scene Two

> (Two hours later.
> Nothing has changed.
> CANANOSA is still sitting on the bench alone.
> A short time after SIL enters, excitedly, with a bouquet
> of flowers in her hand; she is very happy.)

SIL. Oh! I'm so glad. I was afraid you might have gone.

> (Silence)

SIL. Are you cross? It's my fault, I'm sorry. Look, I brought
you some flowers.

CAV. Flowers? I hate flowers.

> (He throws the flowers on the ground and tramples them
> underfoot in a temper.)

SIL. Forgive me, I didn't know you didn't like flowers. I only
wanted to please you.

CAV. You wanted to please me by bringing me flowers?

SIL. Bouquets are pretty.

CAV. And of course nothing suits me better than something
pretty - you just wanted to find the opposite of what I am
and insult me.

SIL. No I only wanted to please you, I swear - you know that.

CAV. Do I? How do I know?

SIL. Because I'm telling you.

CAV. You should have brought me a box-full of manure, you
hear me?

SIL. Yes, I hear you.

CAV. Or better still, a whip. That's a present I'd really have
liked. A whip, to beat you with.

SIL. Do you want me to go and get one?

CAV. No, there's no need.

SIL. You see, I can't do anything right with you.

CAV. What precisely are your intentions?

SIL. I haven't any. I just want to talk to you.

CAV. Just like that, all of a sudden?

SIL. To tell you the truth I was angry when I left you but I
thought about it for a long time and I came to the conclusion
that I just didn't understand you. What must I do to be able
to?

CAV. Commit suicide.

SIL. Can't we ever be friends?

CAV. Friends? You and me, friends?

SIL. Yes.

CAV. You'd be "delighted" as they say, I believe.

SIL. Don't laugh at me.

CAV. I do what I like.

SIL. Have you got a lot of friends?

CAV. Friends? Me? I don't need them, I only have enemies.

SIL. Do you like making enemies?

CAV. Very much!

SIL. Then I'll be your enemy.

CAV. You?

SIL. Yes.

CAV. You don't make the grade.

SIL. I promise you I won't get angry.

CAV. That's no good.

SIL. Tell me what you want me to do and I'll do it. Tell me to buy you a whip so you can beat me and I'll do it.

CAV. (Violently) You're not to talk to me!

SIL. All I ask is that you'll let me stay with you.

(Silence)

CAV. (In another tone of voice) Aren't you afraid of me?

SIL. No.

CAV. I fear the worst.

SIL. What?

CAV. Your friendliness is merely the result of a feeling of "charity". Do you feel sorry for me?

SIL. Not in the least.

CAV. Then tell me why you stay here and talk to me like a friend. Why don't you do what all the others do.

SIL. But they're nothing to do with me.

111

CAV. I'm talking about you.

SIL. I think, as a person, you're quite unique.

(Silence)

CAV. You know, after today, I won't have to imagine all the conversations I might have had with women. After today all I'll have to do is go through the conversation I've had with you in my mind, over and over again.

SIL. But I can go on seeing you, if you've no objection that is.

CAV. Before my life consisted of dreams. Now I have facts.

SIL. It's not good to be alone. Give it up.

CAV. I see now. You're trying to make me lose my virginity. You're <u>making</u> me lose it, you're raping me.

SIL. We're not children.

CAV. I've got other things to do right now, thank you. I'm concentrating on a woman I'm thinking of torturing.

SIL. Are you thinking of any woman in particular.

CAV. Just in general.

SIL. Could it be me?

CAV. Would you agree to it?

SIL. Nobody ever asked me that before.

CAV. If someone had loved you he'd have tied you to the bedrails and whipped you until your body was one gaping wound.

SIL. Is that love?

CAV. Perhaps you'd rather play with me.

SIL. Can't you imagine being happy?

CAV. What are you insinuating? That I'm not happy? What are you trying to say?

SIL. You imply that you're not happy.

CAV. Tell me when.

SIL. All the time.

CAV. Say what you mean, stop being a hypocrite. You think that being what I am, seeing what nature made me, I can't be happy.

SIL. I didn't say anything like that.

CAV. But you implied it. (Violently) It's a lie, a whopping great lie. I am (Shouts) the-happiest-man-on-earth!

SIL. I'm sorry, I still can't seem to do anything right with you. The more I want to be nice to you the less I succeed.

CAV. I don't care whether you're being "nice" or not. You can stuff it up your arse.

SIL. You like insulting me, don't you?

CAV. Yes.

SIL. Go ahead then, insult me.

(They look at each other in silence.
The tension diminishes.)

CAV. Insult you? I'd rather .... I would .... but how do you pay compliments?

SIL. You're laughing at me. You're trying to humiliate me.

CAV. No. If I knew how to say nice things I'd make some up for you.

SIL. Honestly ? Sincerely?

CAV. Honestly, sincerely. I'd tell you I'd like you to come to my home this evening. I'd invite you to sleep on my bed.

SIL. And I'd accept.

CAV. Don't interrupt! What did you interrupt me for?

SIL. You were saying you'd invite me to sleep on your bed.

CAV. Yes, on my bed. And your naked white body would stand out

113

against the black sheets. And I'd gag you hard to stop you
from talking and interrupting me .... And in the morning .... at dawn ....

SIL. What?

CAV. (Poetically) In the morning, dawn's first glimmers would
light up your corpse.

SIL. You want to watch me die.

CAV. No, I want to kill you.

SIL. Why?

CAV. I don't know.

SIL. Would you kiss me before you killed me? Would you sleep
with me?

CAV. No. Not before or after. My lips will never touch yours.
Our genitals will never meet.

SIL. But you said you'd whip me. Would you whip me?

CAV. The ideal thing would be for you to whip yourself, for you
to gag yourself and tie your feet and one hand at least.

SIL. Well, then, I don't leave you completely indifferent, do I?

CAV. Yes, I'd whip you, but not so you could enjoy the pain. I'd
whip you so hard the pain would exceed any pleasure you
might have had. You'd suffer so much you wouldn't be able
to cry.

SIL. But you'd do it, wouldn't you?

CAV. Why me? I'd get one of the servants to do it.

SIL. Would you watch me?

CAV. Do you want to hurt me?

SIL. Why? Did what I said hurt you?

CAV. I don't know .... Your voice .... It all hurts me.
Seeing you, hearing you.

SIL. Tell me your name. I want to remember it and say it.

CAV. I've got an idea. Why don't you call me Quasimodo?

SIL. I'm not insulting you now, am I?

CAV. Don't you think it 's a good idea?

SIL. No.

(Enter the LOVER: Elegant, "Respectably" dressed, well set up with a certain cool assurance. He speaks to SIL.)

LOVER. This is a surprise. I didn't think I'd find you now. I'm sorry but I was tied up with the minister. I just couldn't get here. I had them ring you several times but there was no one at home.

(Silence. She doesn't even look at him.)

LOVER. But .... What's the matter with you?

(Silence)

LOVER. What's the matter with you? Why don't you answer me? Are you angry?

CAV. (To SIL) Tell him: "I'm not in the least angry. "

SIL. (Repeats in the same tone of voice) I'm not in the least angry.

LOVER. What's the meaning of all this?

CAV. (To SIL) This gentleman is a stupid bastard. (He savours the words) I think you'll have to spell it out for him.

LOVER. I didn't know your friends took such liberties with the language.

CAV. (To SIL) The gentleman doesn't think I'm quite respectable.

LOVER (To SIL) Stop being stupid now and come on!

SIL. Please don't touch me -

LOVER. Are you really angry? Because you've been put out?

CAV. The gentleman is not only a (slowly) stupid bastard he's also an optimist.

115

LOVER. Congratulations, you're quite adept with vulgar slang.

CAV. (To SIL) Being a gentleman he knows how to keep calm but being a stupid bastard gentleman he keeps calm in a stupid bastard manner.

LOVER. I can, on occasion, become heated.

CAV. This stupid bastard's trying to threaten me.

LOVER. That's enough. This discussion is no longer interesting. (To SIL) Now, stop behaving like a child and come with me. I couldn't get here any earlier.

SIL. The reason I'm not coming with you is because I prefer to stay with this man.

LOVER. You must be joking of course.

SIL. I feel sorry for you.

LOVER. You want to stay with this tattered remnant of humanity?

SIL. Go away! I don't want to talk to you, I've got nothing to say to you.

CAV. No, no, let him stay, let him stay, I like the way things are going.

LOVER. I don't understand. Are you serious or are you just saying it out of spite?

SIL. Out of spite for what?

CAV. I shall explain. This young lady is staying with me because she likes me better than you. It's possible that should our relationship develop onto a more intimate plane, I may, with considerable indlugence on my part, whip her until her whole body is one streaming wound and then, at day-break, kill her.

LOVER. The man's mad! How can you let him say such things.

SIL. Everything he says is strictly true. I'm his slave.

CAV. (Angry) What does that mean, you whore? You're not my slave.

SIL. I'm sorry.

LOVER. What is all this nonsense?

SIL. You couldn't possibly understand.

LOVER. Yes, I can see it would be quite difficult.

CAV. (Sincere) Why?

LOVER. He's off again.

CAV. (Sincere) No, believe me, honestly, I'm sorry for all the things I said against you.

LOVER. No more sorry than I.

CAV. You see, when there's a woman involved I do everything I can to shine. You follow

LOVER. I understand.

CAV. Believe me, I only insulted you because I realised at once that I was up against a powerful opponent........forgive me for being frank. My bad points frighten me much more than your good ones.

LOVER. I don't think there's any question of rivalry here. After all, we hardly know each other.

CAV. That's right .... and yet I had a nightmare last night and you were in it.

LOVER. How could that be possible when we don't know each other?

CAV. Well, of course, I'm not usually inclined to believe in dreams and omens. But yesterday I had a nightmare. I was one of a series of monsters - I mean misshapen creatures like myself - we were under a tree, with our hands behind our backs and each one of us was attached to one of the branches. The others managed to get free but I was still tied to the tree. Then I saw that the tree had a face like a man, and, as you may have guessed, the man was you.

LOVER. I don't see how you could dream such a thing.

CAV. I agree you don't look like a tyrant. (To SIL) Don't you think he looks like my tyrant though?

SIL. He's of no importance whatsoever.

CAV. (To the LOVER) Let me dream. (Suddenly) Are you sorry for me?

LOVER. Why should I be?

CAV. I won't pursue the matter. I stopped being a homosexual a long time ago.

LOVER. (Ironically) Not thinking of seducing me, are you?

CAV. Could I, I wonder? I'll tell you something. "All my life" -that's what they say, isn't it? - I've dreamed of being a man like you, tall, handsome, in a "smart" suit with a "wonderful" job. No, that's not true, I only dreamed of being handsome and well-built like you.

LOVER. My physical appearance gives me pleasure - is that what you think?

CAV. Let me kiss your hands.

LOVER. This nonsense has gone far enough.

CAV. It isn't nonsense.

(He kisses the LOVER's hands before he can draw them back)

CAV. A kiss of admiration. Everything I've done against you has been a defence against your superiority. Now I'm making good my mistake. I'd sooner admire your superiority, worship it.

LOVER. You're a strange man.

CAV. I'd like so much to watch you at night, furtively, and kiss your hands every day. You'd be my idol, the one thing in life I worshipped.

LOVER. I don't follow.

CAV. Do you want me to dance for you.

(He begins to dance in the most grotesque manner.)

LOVER. Stop, please!

CAV. Am I really so grotesque?

118

LOVER. No, it's not that.

CAV. Shall I sing for you? Shall I sing a song?

LOVER. Please!

CAV. I can see that you find all this display rather vulgar. It cuts against the elegance and refinement of your manners.

LOVER. I'm just not used to it. But, frankly, you do seem a little unbalanced to me.

CAV. You mean I'm mad.

LOVER. I wouldn't go as far as that.

CAV. Of course we musn't overstep the bounds of "good manners".

LOVER. I have the feeling I am wasting my time.

CAV. Do you want to leave with this woman?

LOVER. (To SIL) Let's go.

CAV. Go with him.

SIL. I don't want to go with him.

CAV. Do as you're told!

SIL. I want to stay with you.

LOVER. It seems I'm the villain of the piece.

CAV. Then make the most of it. Enjoy the moment as it happens. It may be the only time you'll ever play the villain. Experience it to the full.

LOVER. (To SIL) Now, I'm speaking quite calmly, will you come with me?

SIL. No, I want to stop here.

LOVER. Then I'm going.

CAV. I think . . . .

LOVER. Be quiet! This is all the result of your scheming.

CAV. Scheming? Then here's the last bit. (To SIL) Go with him.

SIL. Let me stay with you.

CAV. No, you're to go with him and that's an end of it!

SIL. Is that your last word?

CAV. Yes.

SIL. Please ....

CAV. There's no please about it.

SIL. I'll do as you say.

LOVER. You've won all along the line.

CAV. It's all a mistake.

LOVER. At all events my position could hardly be more embarrassing.

CAV. Believe me it's been "an unforgettable evening" .... "You're a gentleman!"

LOVER. You think everything's funny, don't you? We're just playthings in your hands. How are we to know what you're thinking?

CAV. As a person I am an inferior to you.

LOVER. Aren't you sick of this game?

CAV. (Violently) I'm sick of listening to you.

LOVER. You've changed your tone suddenly. What does it mean?

CAV. I don't owe any explanations to you. Clear out! I don't like looking at good, upstanding pigs.

LOVER. Are you insulting me?

CAV. You can hear can't you?

LOVER. If I weren't your .... you deserve a good thrashing.

CAV.   Take one step and I'll skin you alive like a rabbit.

LOVER.   I've never struck a woman and I certainly shan't strike
an invalid.

(Police siren.)

CAV.   Go and fuck this whore in the first hotel you find and leave
me to sleep in peace.

LOVER.   I ought to report you to the police for this unwarrantable
feast of verbal aggression.

CAV.   What's stopping you then? You could kill two birds with one
stone. They're after me for my mother's murder.

LOVER.   I'm not in the least surprised. You criminal! (To SIL)
Let us go!

SIL.   (To CAVANOSA) Come to my place, the police will never
find you there.

LOVER.   You're not going to make yourself an accessory to
murder are you?

SIL.   (To CAVANOSA) Come with me?

CAV.   Don't touch me, you regimental whore!

LOVER.   Your violence will receive its just reward.

CAV.   I'll insult you even when I'm dead.

LOVER.   You're pathetic.

CAV.   Go and take a look at yourself in the mirror, but don't
have a revolver handy because you'll kill yourself when you
see that face of yours - like a down-trodden donkey.

LOVER.   I've heard enough. Coming?

SIL.   No.

LOVER.   Goodbye then.

CAV.   Wait! (To SIL) Go with him. I order you, you whore!

SIL.   Please, let me protect you.

CAV. Go, and I hope the earth opens up and swallows you!

SIL. Please just let me stay a little while.

CAV. I said no!

SIL. I won't say anything. I'll be quiet.

CAV. Clear out!

SIL. Let me stay on that bench over there, I'll be quite a way away.

CAV. I said I hoped the earth would open up and swallow you, didn't you hear? (Shouts) Get out, get out, get out!

(SIL and the LOVER go.
CAVANOSA lies down.
Blackout.)

CAV'S VOICE. Mummy! Mummy!

(Police siren)

Scene Three

(One hour later.
Light reutrns slowly.
Enter SIL. Cavanosa is still stretched out on the bench asleep.
SIL is carrying a whip. She goes up to him slowly and kneels by the bench. SIL watches CAVANOSA for a long time. CAVANOSA suddenly wakes with a start.)

CAV. Mummy, mummy! (Furiously) What are you doing here?

SIL. I had to see you!

CAV. Didn't you hear what I said? Get out!

SIL. Please ....

CAV. There's no please about it!

SIL. I don't want to be a nuisance.

CAV. You're the biggest nuisance I ever met.

SIL. Let me stay here, at your feet, like a cat.

CAV. I suppose you're tired of being fucked by that idiot? Well go and get yourself a "spicy bit of fun".

SIL. I didn't go with him. I went to get you a present .... a whip.

CAV. And is that the best whip you could find?

SIL. I rooted round in the attic and this was all I could find.

CAV. Clear out!

SIL. Take it, please!

CAV. What do you expect me to do with this?

SIL. Beat me. Look, I'll kneel down. Beat me if you like.

CAV. Are you trying to tempt me?

SIL. I only want to see you happy.

CAV. Where do you want me to beat you? On "the palm of your hand" as in school.

SIL. Wherever you like.

CAV. Take your clothes off!

SIL. Here? People can see.

CAV. You want to make me happy don't you?

SIL. I'll do whatever you like.

CAV. Well, go on then!

SIL. What shall I take off first?

CAV. Are you making difficulties?

SIL. Don't get angry. Here.

> (She takes off her blouse then her skirt.
> She takes her shoes off and her stockings followed by her
> slip.)

CAV. Stop! What's all this?

SIL. What's the matter?

CAV. Do you think we're going to play cops and robbers?

SIL. What have I done wrong?

CAV. Look at the whip.

SIL. What's the matter with the whip? Beat me, if you like, I won't try and stop you.

CAV. All that whip would do is tickle you.

SIL. It's leather.

CAV. Where are the barbs?

SIL. Does it need barbs?

CAV. Didn't you know?

SIL. I'll go and get another.

CAV. Fine. Clear out and don't bother to come back.

SIL. Please ....

CAV. What now?

SIL. Let me stay with you a little while.

CAV. What are you after?

SIL. Nothing. I just want to be with you. I wanted to tell you that the police are checking identity papers at all crossroads near here. Let me save you.

CAV. In your panties?

SIL. Whatever way you like.

CAV. What's the sense of all this.

SIL. I'm madly ....

CAV. Spare me your cheap sentiment.

124

SIL. I'll do whatever you tell me.

CAV. Then clear out!

SIL. Please ....

CAV. You want to make me happy, don't you?

SIL. With all my heart.

CAV. Well, you can.

SIL. How?

CAV. By clearing out right now.

SIL. Don't be so hard on me.

CAV. Oh, so I'm supposed to make you happy .... by "making a sacrifice."

SIL. I could go a few steps away and sit on that bench.

CAV. Just let me live my life in peace.

SIL. I'll let you live in peace.

CAV. What are you standing there half naked for?

SIL. You asked me to undress.
CAV. Are you in the habit of undressing every five minutes?

SIL. I've never done it in the street before.

CAV. It's an "indecent act". We could both be sent to prison. Me for "my crime" and -

SIL. I'll hide you at my place.

CAV. I forgot you were a heroine.

SIL. I'm sorry.

CAV. I'm sick of your good manners. What's behind them? (Pause) What have you done with your boy-friend?

SIL. I didn't go with him. He wanted me to go out with him but I went home to get a present for you.

CAV. What did he say about me?

SIL. Well . . . .

CAV. Tell me, you needn't think I'll be outraged.

SIL. Nothing serious. He just warned me to be careful because you were "Mad, and dangerous with it."

CAV. He insulted me?

SIL. As I said, he told me you were mad.

CAV. I was asking if he insulted me, called me a monster or Quasimodo or a stupid-looking cripple.

SIL. I wouldn't have stood for it.

CAV. I really have got quite a bodyguard, haven't I?

SIL. Don't make fun of me.

CAV. Let's put our cards on the table.

SIL. I'm telling the truth.

CAV. Enough of this juvenile sentimentality. Facts! What do you want?

SIL. I've already told you. To stay with you.

CAV. How long for?

SIL. For the rest of my life.

CAV. "The rest of your life". Well, what will you do tonight?

SIL. I'll hide you in my apartment if you'll let me.

CAV. I spend all my time in my room and in the park. No use trying to make me give up my way of life. I couldn't.

SIL. Then I'll come and live with you.

CAV. And the police will arrest me.

SIL. No.

CAV. Suppose everything goes swimmingly and the police don't
arrest me etc........ What will you do with me all day? You
might as well know I don't go to the cinema or the theatre,
I only walk in this park. Would you be able to put up with
that?

SIL. Of course!

CAV. All of it .... "for life"?

SIL. Yes, for life.

CAV. (Angrily) Clear out! Go on clear out! I don't want to see
you again.

(He lies down on the bench face down hands on head.
She stands silently.
She starts to go then comes back.
She goes up to him very cautiously. She kneels down.
She wants to touch him but stops herself.
She looks at him a long time.
She gets up and goes out for a moment.
She comes back and kneels again.)

SIL. Please ....

(She touches him.
Immediately CAVANOSA jumps up in a wild fury. He kicks
her over.)

CAV. How dare you touch me! Me!

(Demented shouts.
He goes to her as she lies on the ground and tramples on
her "savagely".)

CAV. Slut! Whore! Lousy rotten bitch! Take that and that!

(He goes to the bench and kicks the wood.
His fury abates a little.
Then quietly he says: "Mummy   Mummy"
Long silence.
Police siren.
Long silence.
We can hear her weeping "desperately".
Finally she gets up. Her whole body seems to hurt.
She goes to the bench.)

CAV. (Furious again) Don't touch me.

SIL. (Tired) I've come for my clothes.

(She dresses slowly.)

SIL. Can I say goodbye?

(Silence)

SIL. Just let me say how sorry I am we couldn't understand each other.

(Silence)

SIL. Won't you say something to me?

(Silence)

SIL. Just say goodbye. I promise I won't trouble you again, ever.

(Silence)

SIL. If you won't speak to me just nod your head to say goodbye.

(Silence)

SIL. Won't you?

(CAVANOSA tries hard to speak.
She is very impatient. She doesn't say anything waiting for him to speak.
Finally he agrees to say something "as though he had come from another world".

CAV. Why are you going?

SIL. Don't you want me to?

CAV. You realise I could have killed you?

SIL. Yes I could see that from the hate in your face. How could I have made you hate me like that. What crimes must I pay for? Am I just a substitute for the real victim? Why do you hate me so?

CAV. I could have done you a fatal injury.

SIL. Yes.

CAV. Is that why you were going?

SIL. If you hate me so much why should I stay with you?

CAV. You were afraid for your life so you wanted to go. You're not afraid of verbal attack but you are of physical.

SIL. No, believe me I'm not.

CAV. That was the real reason you were running away.

SIL. Believe me . . . .

CAV. Did I frighten you?

SIL. Were you testing me?

CAV. I don't understand.

SIL. You were trying to prove to me I couldn't put up with your violent moods but pretending to have a fit of anger, weren't you?

CAV. Am I a good actor? Did I play my part well?

SIL. Yes, very well. I thought you were very sincere.

CAV. You're wrong. How could I pretend?

SIL. You really meant it then?

CAV. Of course.

SIL. Can I believe you this time?

CAV. Yes.

SIL. Thanks.

(Short silence)

CAV. (In a sincere almost tender voice) Let me dream. Let me believe that everything that's happening is real.

SIL. Tell me.

129

CAV. I don't have to look for a woman any more. She's here for the asking.

SIL. Perhaps I'm not the woman you would have chosen?

CAV. I don't have the luxury of choice. Could I ask for anyone better than you. You're even pretty, aren't you?

SIL. It's not for me to judge.

CAV. I'm not asking you for a subjective judgement. What do other people say about you?

SIL. They're inclined to find me pretty.

CAV. Let me dream, let me dream I'm travelling the world with you. I'd leave my loneliness behind and fling myself into "an adventure". I'd put you in a pram and off we'd go together. And so's you couldn't escape ....

SIL. So's I couldn't escape.

CAV. Let me go on dreaming .... I'd keep you chained up so's you couldn't escape. As we pass through a town I'd lift your skirts so that young men could see your thighs. And at night, before going to sleep, we'd whip each other ....

SIL. You really mean it?

CAV. Yes I do.

SIL. I could help you ....

CAV. If you don't who will?

SIL. Let's travel the world the way you "dreamed" with me chained in this little pram.

CAV. You're making fun of me.

SIL. I mean it.

CAV. Would you be prepared to do it?

SIL. Yes.

CAV. I'm going to ask you a question and I want you to answer me sincerely. How do you find me?

130

SIL. You know.

CAV. (After a long moment's thought) Am I a monster or am I normal?

SIL. (Also thinks) You're not normal.

CAV. Tell me, am I a monster or, if you prefer, an invalid, or a cripple - am I, or not?

SIL. Yes, you are.

CAV. I'm not talking about mental deformities or monstrosities but physical ones, "visible" ones.

(Silence)

CAV. Answer!

SIL. Yes, you are.

CAV. Say: "You're a monster".

SIL. You're deformed.

CAV. All right. What attracts you most about me? My physical appearance or my "spiritual qualities"?

SIL. What can I say?

CAV. The truth.

SIL. Both.

CAV. You're very diplomatic.

SIL. I promised to tell you the truth.

(Silence)

CAV. I'm going to take you home with me to start with.

SIL. Just let me tell you how happy I am.

CAV. I don't know what you're talking about.

SIL. Let me help you.

CAV. A little modesty if you please.

(Police siren)

SIL. They're looking for you.

CAV. How could they have found the body?

SIL. Where is it?

CAV. In my room.

SIL. Wouldn't you rather come to my place?

CAV. I said, let's go to my home.

SIL. Just as you like.

CAV. Will you help me?

SIL. Yes.

CAV. Do you know why I need your help?

SIL. No.

CAV. To carry my mother's body.

SIL. I'll do it for you.

CAV. You'll be taking a great risk.

SIL. I'll do it just the same.

CAV. Remember, your lover warned you.

SIL. I remember.

CAV. You see, it's all got off to a bad start. The body! Doesn't it seem like an omen to you?

SIL. No.

CAV. Let's settle the first thing right now. You'll wait for me on the pavement outside. When everything's clear and you can come up I'll signal with the light three times from my balcony then I'll switch off. It's that balcony there. See it?

SIL. The first or the second.

132

CAV. The second. See it? You go into No. 15. It's first on the left. Give several sharp taps and I'll open.

SIL. What do you mean by "signal with the light three times"?

CAV. I'll switch on and off three times. If I leave the light on don't come up. It means there's danger.

SIL. This is to be my final humiliation, isn't it? You'll keep me waiting until dawn, won't you?

CAV. No.

(He goes.)

SIL. Bye. See you soon.

CURTAIN

ACT ONE

(Darkness.
 A few minutes later.)

(CAVANOSA's Room.
 Several naked female dolls, life size.
 A bed.
 Two doors.
 A balcony.)

(CAVANOSA enters.
 Goes to one of the dolls kisses and caresses it.
 Goes to the bed and covers it with an eiderdown so as to
 hide something which we cannot quite see in the darkness.
 He goes to the balcony and looks out into the street. He
 flicks the light twice. As he is going to switch off for the
 second time he realises that his mother is sitting at a small
 table playing patience.
 He leaves the light on.)

MOTHER. (Hides her eyes) Put the light out, darling. It hurts
my eyes.

CAV. What are you doing?

MOTHER. I was waiting for you.

CAV. I told you not to come into my room!

MOTHER. Can't a mother come into her son's room any more?

CAV. You know I don't like it.

MOTHER. Don't be such a baby. Give me a kiss. Come on, give
me a kiss and don't be so naughty. All you think about are
your dolls. You're with them all the time, day and night.
Well, aren't you going to give me a kiss?

134

(He goes to her and kisses her very coldly.)

MOTHER. What a son I've got!

CAV. Why don't you go to bed?

MOTHER. Let me get this game out. But first of all, let me
look at you .... You're my son.

CAV. I wanted to do some work.

MOTHER. Can I help you, darling?

CAV. It's private.

MOTHER. Darling, do you remember how happy we used to be?
You were a quiet child and I used to take you to the park
after all the other children had gone, so they couldn't shout
rude things after you. You used to trot along. Remember?

CAV. "Yes".

MOTHER. You never go out in the evening's with me now.

CAV. It's not the same any more.

MOTHER. You're a "Man" now, aren't you?

CAV. I'm not a little boy any longer.

MOTHER. Do you remember what you used to do?

CAV. "Yes".

MOTHER. Remember? You used to make garlands with leaves
from the trees and crown me with them.

CAV. "Yes".

MOTHER. And you said that when you were grown up you'd put
me in a pram so I wouldn't get tired and you'd travel the
whole world with me. You'd show everyone how beautiful
I was. Remember? You used to tell me I was beautiful.

CAV. Of course I remember. Why are you telling me all this
tonight?

MOTHER. Because I know that tonight you want to kill me. I'm

135

not wrong am I?

CAV. What are you talking about?

MOTHER. Darling, be very careful. Do it discreetly. The police are very astute these days.

CAV. Can't you talk about something else?

MOTHER. It's high time I was in bed, though .... How many times nights fell suddenly while we were in the park or your room, and took us by surprise!

CAV. While you were whipping me.

MOTHER. It was for your own good. I didn't want you to turn into a little hooligan. Now, you're going to blame me for ....

CAV. I'm not blaming you for anything.

MOTHER. It all started with those dolls. What did you want dolls for when you've got me? I should never have bought them for you. That's how, bit by bit, you drew away from me.

CAV. Are we going to have another string of complaints?

MOTHER. No darling. I want you to be happy. I've only ever thought of you, ever since the day you were born. Who protected you when your classmates used to sing rude songs at you and call you Quasimodo? I was always there with you, to look after you and keep you from harm. If I whipped you sometimes it was only to check your worst side.

CAV. That was why you used to chain me sometimes.

MOTHER. It was our special game. When I used to whip you it was partly a game. You're not going to blame me <u>now</u>, are you?

CAV. I ....

MOTHER. Believe me, it all started with those dolls. I should never have allowed it. At first it was just normal size doll, then, each time they got bigger, till now they're life size. You wouldn't have any other kind. No more talk about going round the world in a pram.

CAV. You wouldn't understand.

136

MOTHER. Wouldn't understand what?

CAV. My .... desires.

MOTHER. I'm a human being like you. Go on, tell me.

CAV. I don't know how to explain.

MOTHER. I'm too old to understand, I suppose?

CAV. No, it's not that.

MOTHER. Good. Don't tell me anything, it's probably better that way. I'd much rather you didn't do anything to hurt me. (Pause) What can you find elsewhere that I can't give you? Not many mothers would have gone to the lengths I have.

CAV. I don't think you should ever have let me go to the park. You should have shut me up at the back of the house where I couldn't see the street. I shouldn't have seen anyone but you - no maids, no servants, just you -.

MOTHER. I never thought of that. How many times I've been sorry for it since. It would have been the perfect union, unique.

CAV. Still, I've never seen many people.

MOTHER. It was a mistake to send you to school.

CAV. You can say that again.

MOTHER. It wasn't because they shouted rude things at you - that was inevitable seeing the way you're deformed - no, because of all the harm that can still come from it. You started seeing people. Up till then we'd lived alone. Even the doctor didn't see you. I told him what was wrong with you and he explained the treatment.

CAV. "The good old days".

MOTHER. They were the best days.

CAV. Don't remind me of the past.

MOTHER. Now you're full of delusions of grandeur, fantasies, plans for the future. What are you after? What are you trying to find? You won't be happy with anyone but me.

137

CAV. I'm not denying it.

MOTHER. Come back to the fold. We'll start all over again as though nothing had happened.

CAV. It's not possible any more.

MOTHER. (Uneasily) Have you lost your virginity?

CAV. No, never!

MOTHER. You go around in such a daydream these days it wouldn't surprise me if you did anything stupid.

CAV. Not that though.

MOTHER. Don't forget, darling, those sort of things can always be avoided. I've shown you how. I am always here, ready to -

CAV. (Cutting in) Your hands, mother ....

MOTHER. (Cutting in) You mean I'm an old woman?

CAV. No.

MOTHER. Can't you be content with me?

CAV. What a question!

MOTHER. And I've just got to get used to the way you make a fuss over those dolls.

CAV. They're mine.

MOTHER. I bought them though.

CAV. Well, now they're mine. They never talk! And they're always smiling.

MOTHER. I love you, don't I?

CAV. Oh, please! We're back on that again!

MOTHER. I'm yours, aren't I? I smile, don't I?

CAV. "Yes" "You too".

MOTHER. The way you said that!
138

CAV. How am I supposed to say it?

MOTHER. Sincerely?

CAV. More sincerely?

MOTHER. I've never said anything to you but do you know something?

CAV. What?

MOTHER. Sometimes - because I love you so very, very much, - I've watched you when you were alone in your room.

CAV. And you saw me crying, didn't you?

MOTHER. And other things too.

CAV. You heard me calling for you?

MOTHER. Yes, I heard you calling for me, as though you were dreaming, as though you were crying.

CAV. Just a reflex action. You shouldn't take it too literally.

MOTHER. But you were calling for me.

CAV. They were for my "mother".

MOTHER. I'm your mother, aren't I?

CAV. They were for the mother I had when I was a child. I used to wait in bed, in the evening, with all the lights out, until you came and kissed me.

MOTHER. I'm still the same person.

CAV. It wasn't the same.

MOTHER. That's it, make out I'm an old woman!

CAV. Why?

MOTHER. Hurt me, scratch me, widen this gaping wound in my heart - pitilessly.

CAV. Let's not go into melodrama, if you don't mind.

MOTHER. Darling, it's true, there is a wound in my heart. Call

it what you like. I'm not "modern" like you. I can only
talk in the words my poor parents taught me and they were
even more old-fashioned than I am.

CAV. Change the record. We know it.

MOTHER. You know them all. I've never hidden anything from
you (Pause) Darling, I saw you doing certain things while
you were shut in your room and you still haven't "guessed"
what I'm talking about.

CAV. What then?

MOTHER. The dolls.

CAV. What about my dolls?

MOTHER. Don't you know?

CAV. Tell me.

MOTHER. What do you do with them?

CAV. I play.

MOTHER. What at?

CAV. I just - play.

MOTHER. Don't you kiss them sometimes?

CAV. Oh, please.

MOTHER. You kiss your dolls. I saw you. I watched you very
carefully. You have different favourites - you change them
every so often. At the moment it's this one. (She indicates
one of the dolls) I'm right, aren't I?

CAV. What are you getting at?

MOTHER. I want you to know that I've seen you kiss them
"passionately".

CAV. I'm entitled to. They're mine.

MOTHER. There's more love in it when you kiss them than when
you kiss your mother.

CAV. Possibly.

MOTHER. So you admit it?

CAV. Yes, I admit it.

MOTHER. You talk to them as well, you tell them your secrets.

CAV. It's a game.

MOTHER. And when you kiss them you fondle them. Is that a game, too?

CAV. Yes.

MOTHER. Is it a game when you stroke their stomachs and put their hands on yours. Is that a game, too?

CAV. Let me alone. Please, don't talk to me.

MOTHER. You don't like the sound of the truth. You'd much rather I had to watch the absurd spectacle of my son being fondled by a doll's hands, and then justify it.

CAV. I don't have to justify myself.

(Silence)

MOTHER. How you've changed!

CAV. You don't leave me chained up in the cellar three nights at a stretch any more, because I'd done something stupid, do you? That's a change isn't it?

MOTHER. You know very well that I can still do it, and I shall.

CAV. Only when I let you.

MOTHER. "Now you're a man, an adult".

CAV. Now I'm your accomplice when I feel like it.

MOTHER. How could you prefer a doll's hands to mine? How you've changed. I'd never have imagined it. You were always so obedient, always ready to do what I wanted .... but now ....

CAV. It's time to go to bed.

MOTHER. And what were you doing between the sheets with that one? (Indicating another doll) I suppose I must fear the worst?

CAV. I didn't do what you're thinking.

MOTHER. As if it mattered. Instead of making a hole, you just squeezed her thighs together.

CAV. It's not true. And never will be.

MOTHER. You just used your hands.

CAV. Yes.

MOTHER. Well, that's a relief.

CAV. You want me to be a virgin and I always shall be.

MOTHER. Darling, think of me a little more. I've always looked after you and petted you. You've got such delicate lungs. At the first sign of a cold I've always been at your bedside, applying poultices. Look at that scraggy regiment of weaklings. What could they do for you? Tell me you love me.

CAV. You know I love you.

MOTHER. That's what you say .... but I've often seen you doing things for other people you'd never do for me. With me you're passive: with them you're active. Look at that doll, and that one, and that. (Pointing to them) Turn them round, with their backs to us, away from the wall.

CAV. Say it.

MOTHER. Do you think I go around with my head in the clouds?

CAV. Tell me everything you want to say.

MOTHER. You mean you don't care?

CAV. No, but I want to go to bed.

MOTHER. Hypocrite!

CAV. Why?

MOTHER. I'm talking about your dolls and you tell me you're sleepy.

142

CAV. I promise you I don't know who they are. At various times I think about one or two of them and forget the others.

MOTHER. Have you forgotten that you whipped these three until they were all tattered and torn? Have you forgotten that?

CAV. I remember now.

MOTHER. And I'll tell which whip it was with. This one!

(She points to a whip on the chest of drawers.)

CAV. Yes, that's right. The dolls are mine.

MOTHER. And have you forgotten you're keeping this one chained up? (Points to it) Have you forgotten?

CAV. No.

MOTHER. What has she done wrong?

CAV. Why are you asking?

MOTHER. She's done nothing wrong. You just wanted to see her suffer the way you suffered.

CAV. Because you tortured me.

MOTHER. I tortured you for your own good. Because I loved you!

CAV. I love her, too.

MOTHER. And you loved me too, didn't you? You just told me, didn't you?

CAV. Yes.

MOTHER. But you never chained me up or beat me.

CAV. I didn't dare.

MOTHER. With her you dared.

CAV. Anyway you wouldn't have liked it.

MOTHER. How do you know?

CAV. I never thought of that.

143

MOTHER. (Change of tone, sweetly) Poor darling. Always running out to find what you already have at home. A mother is a martyr, she only lives for her son. Get that idea into your head. Love me and let me love you. We could be the happiest couple in the world. I'll look after you, feed you, do everything. I sacrificed my life and my youth for you. You've never seen me going out, looking for distractions this way and that. All my life I've been your slave, attentive to your slightest whims. Come here darling. Sit on my lap as you did when you were nice. Don't be sulky. Let me spoil you and dandle you.

(She sits him on her knees.)

MOTHER. I'm so happy to know that you're near to my heart, sitting on my lap. I want to dream, imagine a life where we'd be together always in this room.

CAV. Mother . . . .

MOTHER. Don't say anything. Just let me speak. You just listen and relax. You must be tired. Every night you go to bed at God knows what time, and God knows where you've been. You've got black rings round your eyes. Are you ill? Do you feel all right?

CAV. A bit tired.

MOTHER. You're always so busy, running here there and everywhere looking for God knows what. One day you'll be as old and as wise as I am. You'll know then that life can't give you what you want, and that all the things you want to know and experience are only bad for you. You're not like other people, you know that. I've never hidden your bad side from you, or your good. Besides, you're highly strung, you might do something really silly. You should keep a watch on yourself. When you get carried away you do the most irresponsible things. Not so very long ago, before you started going out every night, I was the only person in the world you loved and there wasn't anything you wouldn't do for me. One day you climbed up on the roof to get some tiles, stole them, and made a throne for me. Remember?

CAV. Yes, I remember.

MOTHER. You might have fallen from the roof and been smashed to pieces. Another time you went off to the cemetery - I don't know how you managed it, you never would tell me - but you brought me back a little white coffin. Now I think of it

.... You loved me so much! Do you love me still?

CAV. It's not the same thing.

MOTHER. Tell me the truth. You love me a lot less now.

CAV. It's not the same.

MOTHER. Darling, you're so cruel to me.

CAV. Let me alone.

(He gets up)

MOTHER. Tell me I'm being a nuisance.

CAV. I want to sleep, I want ....

MOTHER. Say it then. "I want to be alone".

CAV. Mother!

MOTHER. Do you remember? Not so long ago you used to hid on top of the wardrobe, like a cat, just to watch me walking around when "I thought I was alone" - that's what you said. Remember?

CAV. Yes.

MOTHER. Who'd have thought a few dolls would make you lose all sense?

CAV. You started it, you bought me a doll.

MOTHER. Because you asked me to. And I bought a normal sized doll.

CAV. You were crazy about that little doll. You used to talk to it some like some old maid talking to her diddums.

MOTHER. It was you, you were crazy about her. You used to talk to her and tell her your secrets and quarrel with her. You said she was "sulky" or "happy". She was the first person you'd ever spoken to in your life apart from me.

CAV. (Dreamily) She was very strange.

MOTHER. You made a world for her, and you gave her a little

coffin, just like you did to me.

CAV. (Dreamily) What was it I called her?

MOTHER. How should I know?

CAV. You see, I've even forgotten what I used to call her.

MOTHER. You replaced her with another one, a bigger one, and I know why.

(She goes to the chest of drawers and takes out a small coffin.)

MOTHER. What's in this coffin?

CAV. The little doll.

(She opens the coffin. The little Doll appears with its head torn off.)

MOTHER. Why's she got her head torn off?

CAV. I was playing and . . . .

MOTHER. I saw you squeezing her head while you were having a violent quarrel.

CAV. Poor little dolly.

MOTHER. Are you going to start crying?

CAV. Can't I miss her a little?

MOTHER. You miss her so much you're about to start crying.

CAV. I was very fond of her. I had to kill her.

MOTHER. Darling, poor darling, you're so unhappy!

CAV. You taught me how to be.

MOTHER. I tried to make you happy.

CAV. You treated me like a monster.

MOTHER. But you are a monster.

CAV. I'm not a monster.

146

MOTHER. Look in the mirror.

CAV. What will the mirror tell me?

MOTHER. It'll tell you what you are.

CAV. I'm what you made me. I came out of your womb. I'm your child.

MOTHER. Is that my fault?

CAV. Of course.

MOTHER. How was I to know my son would be a monster?

CAV. (Shouting) I'm not a monster! I'm not a monster! I'm not a monster!

MOTHER. What are you then?

CAV. I have one or two physical defects, that's all. Would you mind very much if I were normal?

MOTHER. To hear such a thing at my age, after all I've done for you.

CAV. You've always tried to make me think I wasn't like other people, that I was ludicrous.

MOTHER. If you weren't so ludicrous why do you think the boys at school made fun of you and shouted rude things at you?

CAV. Kids are like that.

MOTHER. But they only said them to you, not anyone else.

CAV. That makes you very happy! Fine, you've won.

MOTHER. It's a failure, my biggest failure. It's all your father's fault.

CAV. Are you going to drag that up again?

MOTHER. You didn't know him. He was repellent, a monster.

CAV. You've told me a thousand times.

MOTHER. And believe me you take far more after him than you

147

do after me.

CAV. If he was so repellent why did you marry him?

MOTHER. He was strangely "attractive".

CAV. So you can be monstrous, like my father, and still lead a normal life and marry a pretty girl like you.

MOTHER. I was the prettiest of them all. In those days - tastes have changed so much - men used to fight over me.

CAV. But you went away with him.

MOTHER. He was so clever. He knew how to manage things. He was a disgusting man!

CAV. Disgusting?

MOTHER. He knew just the right words to use, to offset his physical appearance. What an actor!

CAV. And you believed his act?

MOTHER. Quite blindly!

CAV. Was it really an act?

MOTHER. Of course. I was his plaything. He was inhumanly selfish towards me. All he wanted was one thing, to experiment, to see how far he could go. I was just a child in those days, with a head full of romantic dreams.

CAV. So it was a romantic adventure.

MOTHER. Yes, of course.

CAV. A wild passionate love.

MOTHER. If you like.

CAV. You see ....

MOTHER. But only because he was so clever.

CAV. Then there's still hope for me. Why keep me shut in the house? Why stop me seeing anyone? Why can't I go out and pick the prettiest girl and seduce her?

148

MOTHER. You lack experience. You don't know how to say things the way he did.

CAV. I'm not as good as him.

MOTHER. On the contrary. You're more innocent.

CAV. There's no hope for me, is there?

MOTHER. You're so excitable! Believe me, darling, whichever way it went, if you were Apollo in person, you wouldn't ever be happy in the world. Break what ties you have and stay with me. To me you're the most adorable creature in the whole world. I like you just as you are - that's why I don't hide the truth from you. Look at me, darling! Do you realise we're just hurting each other with all this talk.

CAV. I want to go to bed.

MOTHER. That's it! I'm in the way, you want to get rid of me! You're not the same as you used to be.

CAV. Things change ....

MOTHER. You've changed. I haven't.

CAV. Was he like me?

MOTHER. Who?

CAV. My father.

MOTHER. Yes and no. You have the same features but there's something, I don't know, that makes you completely different.

CAV. In what way was he clever?

MOTHER. He was so subtle with it. He always gave the impression that everything was above board, no tricks. He pretended to say more than was strictly true. He never hesitated to show himself in the most unfavourable light, boasting he had the most terrible vices. It was a kind of seduction in reverse, putting everything that was low and horrible about him into strong relief. You'd have said he was so vulnerable, so lonely .... He seemed to need affection. I was a child, still tied to my mother's apron strings. I had no experience. I was easily taken in by him.

CAV. When did you realise the truth?

MOTHER. Later on. I got to know him. And I know you, too -
you're so close to the original. I could tell from your look,
as soon as you came in, that you wanted to kill me.

CAV. Don't say that!

MOTHER. Don't be afraid of words and not of actions. Recognise
the truth. Say it! Isn't it true you wanted to kill me?

CAV. (Dreamily) Yes, I want to with all my soul.

MOTHER. My poor darling, the depths to which you have fallen!
How could you possibly hate me that much?

CAV. I'm sick of the sight of you!

MOTHER. Have you thought about it carefully? You really have
made up your mind?

CAV. Yes.

MOTHER. You've done all the necessary?

CAV. Everything.

MOTHER. And you're the one who always calls me as soon as
you're awake, you call out in your sleep "Mummy! Mummy!"
My poor darling child.

(Long pause. She vainly waits for her son to console her.)

MOTHER. What do you want to kill me with?

CAV. A knife.

MOTHER. Show me, I want to see it.

(He takes a long knife from his trousers.)

MOTHER. That's what I was afraid of. A knife .... Five
hours to die! And this is how you treat your own mother!

(As he turns he tries to stab her in the back but he does not
dare. His MOTHER sees what has happened and turns her
back.)

MOTHER. (In a frenzy) Strike me! Strike me! Strike!

(She turns her back to the "sacrifice" he raises the knife

150

but does not dare to strike.)

MOTHER.   (In a frenzy) Go on, go on! Kill me once and for all!
        Coward!

(He tries once more but does not dare. His MOTHER drops
breathless, into an armchair on the verge of hysterics.
Exhausted he also sits.
They both stay this way for a long while in solence.
Suddenly his MOTHER begins to cry "fit to break her heart".)

MOTHER.   I'm so unhappy! I'm so unhappy!

(More tears.
 She calms down.
 Long silence.)

MOTHER.   (Through her tears) Why didn't you dare my baby?

(Long silence.)

MOTHER.   You should have had done with me, darling. There's
        still time. Is it the light that's stopping you? Shall I turn it
        out?

(Silence)

MOTHER.   Let's go up to the attic. You can kill me in the attic.
        It's dark up there.

(Silence.
 She weeps again.)

MOTHER.   (Through her tears) I'm so unhappy! I'm so unhappy!

(She weeps.
 Long silence.)

MOTHER.   (Trying to control herself and finally succeeding) I
        musn't pay too much attention to my own feelings. I must
        be strong. So, my dear boy, you will kindly not kill me with
        a knife but strike me a heavy blow on the head with the cand-
        elabra. Like that I shall lose consciousness immediately. I
        don't want any pain. Just one more piece of advice, for your
        own sake. Go very carefully. Don't get yourself arrested. I
        don't want you to spend the rest of your life in prison.

CAV.   I'm going, forever.

MOTHER. You're leaving everything? Me .... the house ......
perhaps one day you might even manage to get rid of yourself. We'll see.

CAV. I will.

MOTHER. I hope you can, dearest. Believe me I want it with all
my heart. I'm quite resigned to it. If you don't want to live
with me it's better you should go your own way, even if it
means breaking your poor mother's heart.

CAV. Now you're the one who's being clever.

MOTHER. No, my dear boy, I'm tired of life. I haven't the
strength to fight any more. I give up the struggle.

CAV. Good.

MOTHER. Give me a kiss before I leave you.

CAV. A kiss? After all that's happened?

MOTHER. Yes. A farewell kiss.

CAV. (Tired) As you like.

(They kiss ceremoniously.)

MOTHER. (Clinging to him) No, not like that, kiss me tenderly.

CAV. Let me go. I want to be the one to kiss you.

MOTHER. (Violently) Kiss me!

CAV. Let me go, you're hurting. You're digging your nails into
me.

MOTHER. I'm your mother.

CAV. You'll draw blood with your nails.

MOTHER. You're my prisoner. You can't do anything against me,
can you? Eh?

CAV. Let me go!

MOTHER. I want to kiss you first.

CAV. You're hurting.

152

MOTHER. Now I'm in charge of operations. Try and rebel.

CAV. Mother!

MOTHER. That's it, be humble, grovel. Say you're sorry for everything.

CAV. "Sorry".

MOTHER. Say it better than that. Say, "I'm very sorry, mummy darling".

CAV. Do I have to?

MOTHER. (Violently) Did you hear what I said?

(He yells. Doubtless his MOTHER has just hurt him even more.)

MOTHER. Say it properly.

CAV. "I'm very sorry, mummy darling."

MOTHER. Now, I'm going to kiss you.

(She kisses her son on the lips. He yells. Blood spurts from his lips. She lets him go. He takes out a handkerchief and wipes his lips.)

CAV. Look what you've done. You bit me. You didn't want to kiss me you wanted to hurt me.

MOTHER. Shall I put salt and vinegar on it?

CAV. To hurt me even more?

MOTHER. To prevent infection.

CAV. I'm used to it.

MOTHER. None of your wounds has ever become infected, thanks to all the care I've taken. Let me just put a little salt and vinegar on it.

CAV. Stay away from me.

MOTHER. Are you afraid of me?

CAV. (Thinks) Yes.

153

MOTHER. How well nature does things! I'm not only stronger than you mentally but physically as well. You're just a poor cripple with no strength in you. And mentally you're just a poor thing without any experience at all.

CAV. Here endeth the first lesson.

MOTHER. I shall go on showing you the right path.

CAV. I've had enough of you.

MOTHER (Violently) Don't rebel against me! Don't raise your voice to your mother. (Silence) That's right. Be quiet and listen to me.

(Long silence.)

MOTHER. Darling, you see how disagreeable you force me to be? I'm the sort of mother who hangs on her son's least whim, I'm a loving mother. I'm so wretched and unhappy! Life is so cruel to me! How have I offended against God?

CAV. That's it. Mix up our business with your rotten God who punishes sinners and rewards those who do "good deeds".

MOTHER. Now that you're leaving me how could I manage without God?

CAV. I want to get away from all these myths, these horrible myths!

MOTHER. Don't blaspheme.

CAV. I'm not. That disgusting load of filth you call God doesn't exist, that's all.

MOTHER. That's it, mount the horse of Attila. Ride rough-shod over everything I hold most dear. My love for you is so great I don't mind being trampled on if it will make you happy. Ever since you were a tiny baby it's always been my ....

CAV. Don't let's go through the family album.

MOTHER. How you hate it when I tell you about the times in our life when we loved each other most.

CAV. Look to the future.

MOTHER. I'm not as "modern" as you. I'm just a poor woman

154

with no education.

CAV. What's that got to do with it?

MOTHER. Don't treat me like that, darling, even if it's only because of my white hair.

CAV. I know that song too.

MOTHER. Hurt me, be ruthless.

CAV. It's you who hurt me.

(He takes out his handkerchief: it is bloodstained.)

MOTHER. You exasperated me.

CAV. I never know when and why you get exasperated. When I was younger I loved you so much but you still used to hurt me and you can't say that I exasperated you then.

MOTHER. I wanted you to grow up decently.

CAV. Decently ... so you could take advantage.

MOTHER. I won't allow you to say that. When have you ever seen me indulge myself? I've sacrificed my whole life to you. You know how much I like going to the theatre but I haven't been once since you were born because I didn't want you to be left alone at night.

CAV. And these days I ask you to leave me alone and you stay.

MOTHER. Why all the hurry for me to go? Tell me. Who are you expecting?

CAV. Nobody.

MOTHER. You've changed so much I believe you really could go out with someone. Tell me, have you got any friends?

CAV. No.

MOTHER. You musn't believe anyone. There are no such things as friends. They'll scramble up a bit higher over your dead body at the first opportunity.

CAV. You've told me that a thousand times already.

MOTHER. What about women? Have you got any women, darling?

CAV. No.

MOTHER. You have to be very careful. These days they're quite
capable of keeping your company just to deceive you and get
money out of you ....

CAV. "Never for love's sake."

MOTHER. I'm a woman and I've a lot of experience; all women
want is money. Be very careful darling. Modern women
are very dangerous. These days you can see them naked
almost anywhere. Those sluts are capable of anything. There's
an old book I seem to remember where it says that one day men
men will be pursued by women and will have to climb up into
trees to get away from them. That day has come.

(Long silence.)

MOTHER. Why do you tell me lies?

CAV. Do I?

MOTHER. Then tell me again you haven't any friends.

CAV. I haven't any friends.

MOTHER. You don't know anybody, right?

(Silence
She goes to the balcony.)

MOTHER. (Angrily) So who's that little whore down there looking
up here so anxiously.

CAV. I don't know.

MOTHER. I don't believe it.

CAV. I don't know anything about her .... her name or where
she comes from, nothing.

MOTHER. I believe you. A whore has no name.

CAV. "I do not know her profession".

MOTHER. And how much is she going to get from you to let you
sleep with her? (Pause) No, of course. They're much too

156

crafty to talk about that yet.

CAV. If you're trying to hurt her you're going the wrong way about it.

MOTHER. I'm a fool, innocent as the day I was born. Any feeble little thing can take my poor son in, better than I can. I don't want us to quarrel, darling. I'm sorry I lost my temper. I ask your pardon with all my heart.

(Silence)

MOTHER. Did you hear me, darling? I ask your pardon with all my heart.

(Silence)

MOTHER. Tell me you forgive me darling. I promise I'll change. I'll be just what you want me to be. Give me some hope.

CAV. I'm listening.

MOTHER. Don't be unkind and unnatural. You know how weak I am. You know what an effort everything is. I'm ill. My blood pressure's high. I get out of breath coming upstairs. I can't walk very far any more.

CAV. I'm ill too.

MOTHER. But what a difference there is between us! I'll die soon. And it'll be your fault. You're roasting me over a slow fire. If you go to this woman I don't know if my heart will stand it. The doctor told me I had the first signs of encephalitis, brought on by frustration. I didn't say anything because I didn't want him to know you were the cause of my frustrations. Kill me if you want, kill me with your own hands but don't let me die slowly of misery. What a cross I have to bear! I have passed every station. (Pause) I saw how you behaved with with that woman last night.

CAV. You've no right to spy on me.

MOTHER. Don't think I do it for pleasure. If you know how I suffered to see all the kinds of subterfuge you used to do to get what you wanted.

CAV. Mother!

MOTHER. That's it, call me mother. Love me.

157

CAV. Not any more!

MOTHER. Why? At least pretend.

CAV. I don't know how to pretend.

MOTHER. How ironical. I heard every word you said to that girl.
You don't know how to pretend! Darling .... (Sweetly)
Why did you tell her you'd killed me?

CAV. I don't know.

MOTHER. You wanted to get used to the idea.

CAV. Perhaps.

MOTHER. And perhaps you needed her to help you ....

CAV. Why couldn't I do it by myself?

MOTHER. You've just proved you can't.

CAV. I didn't want to.

MOTHER. Spare me this final humiliation. By yourself, yes. With
her help, no. One day you'll realise that I'm the only person
who has any claim on you because I'm the only one ever to
love you with all their heart. I want you just as you are,
exactly as you are. Do try and understand.

CAV. I do.

(Long silence)

CAV. I've been thinking about the past, too. (With conviction) I
know that with you I've been as happy as it's possible to be. You
You reminded me of things we did, and I could remind you of
some you've forgotten. I remember I was jealous of everybody. When we used to go out I used to stick a stupid notice
on your back to stop the men coming near you. And when
people used to laugh you thought it was because of me and
the way I looked, and we were happy.

MOTHER. You loved me so much, my darling!

CAV. Yes, mother, and I know that love is lost and gone for ever.
You see, I'm quite sincere about it. But I also have to tell
that I cannot and will not live with you any longer. I dream of
travelling, of going ....

158

MOTHER. Nothing's ever that definite. Change your mind. Come back.

CAV. It's impossible. (Pause) Perhaps it's possible.

MOTHER. Yes.

CAV. But if I stay .... how could we find what we had?

MOTHER. We could do it.

CAV. I was a child.

MOTHER. You weren't. How old were you when you used to write strange things I couldn't understand on the lavatory paper, to surprise me? How old were you then? Do you remember?

CAV. 23.

MOTHER. You see? You weren't a child any longer! And at that same period, remember? You used to make little birds out of silver paper and put them all over my body while I pretended to be asleep. Another time - later this was - you didn't want me to go out without you, and when you saw me getting ready to go you nailed your hand to the front door and threatened to stay there till I came back.

CAV. There's no point in going on. This woman and I are going to live together.

MOTHER. I don't believe it.

CAV. I intend living with her.

MOTHER. Tell me it's not true.

CAV. I don't want to deceive you. It's the truth.

MOTHER. Then I only want to ask you one thing, my darling. Bring her here to live.

CAV. And if she refuses?

MOTHER. You think I don't know you both, your father and you? "If she refuses" .... as if she'll have anything to say in the matter! You'll do the deciding.

CAV. Why do you want me to stay here. So you can spy on me all the time?

159

MOTHER. I'll do whatever you ask.

CAV. I know you.

MOTHER. I'll even do whatever she asks. I'll be her slave. I'll polish her shoes every day and do all the cooking.

CAV. She'd rather have her freedom.

MOTHER. And you?

CAV. I would too.

MOTHER. I'm rejected then. (Pause) Bring her up here, now, so I can have a closer look at her.

CAV. Go away then.

MOTHER. You want me to go away! What lies are you going to tell her?

CAV. I don't intend telling her any.

MOTHER. You'll tell her the truth about your dolls?

CAV. Of course.

MOTHER. You mean, you'll tell her "everything".

CAV. What do you mean?

MOTHER. You won't keep anything hidden from her?

CAV. No. In fact I'll tell her the worst things I can think of.

MOTHER. I know that trick! (Pause) But I know there are certain things you won't tell her.

CAV. You're hiding something. Tell me.

MOTHER. No, you're hiding something.

CAV. Tell me.

MOTHER. Are you going to tell her you were with another woman last night?

CAV. How do you know that?

MOTHER. There's not much a mother doesn't know, not when it comes to her son.

CAV. Especially if "she spends her time spying like a lousy copper."

MOTHER. Aren't you ashamed?

CAV. Of you?

MOTHER. That I should know you were with another woman yesterday.

CAV. Not at all.

MOTHER. You swore "eternal love" to her?

CAV. It was an old maid I found in chruch.

MOTHER. You go to church?

CAV. I went to church to see if I could find a woman.

MOTHER. And you told her lies, to seduce her.

CAV. "I told her lies".

MOTHER. The things that can happen! The worry of it! Go out and pick up the first woman you see.

CAV. (Shouts) That's it. The first one you see!

MOTHER. Don't get into a temper.

CAV. It's your fault.

MOTHER. "Mine" of course!

CAV. That's right, yours. You always made me think I was a monster.

MOTHER. (Authoritarian) Be quiet! You hear?

(Long silence)

MOTHER. (Different tone) I'm so unhappy! So unhappy!

(Long silence)

MOTHER. I won't say anything hurtful, my darling. As you want this woman I'd like you to remember me nicely. Say it to me darling.

CAV. Yes, mother.

MOTHER. I like it when you talk like that! Do you think we could still get on together?

CAV. Yes.

MOTHER. How I wish you were a homosexual! Then I'd have had to fight a man. They're purer than women. They don't think about your money.

CAV. Have you got what you wanted now?

MOTHER. Don't reproach me, darling. You see I know all your little tricks but I don't say anything.

CAV. You've said quite enough already.

MOTHER. For instance. What's that on the bed?

(She goes towards the bed. He steps in the way.)

CAV. Don't touch my bed!

MOTHER. What are you afraid of? Tell me what's under the eiderdown?

(She gets past her son and lifts a corner of the eiderdown. Legs are seen. He hides them.)

MOTHER. Legs.

CAV. Yes, legs.

MOTHER. Woman's legs.

CAV. No, doll's legs.

MOTHER. You've got beyond the doll stage now. You go much further now.

CAV. Let me alone. Go away!

MOTHER. Very well, darling. I shan't wait for you to say it a second time. I'm going. But just tell me first: Is there any-

162

thing you want, the two of you? I should so like to help you
both to be happy!

CAV. Let me alone.

MOTHER. Aren't you going to kiss me?

CAV. Are you going to start again?

MOTHER. Darling, kiss me.

(He kisses her. MOTHER goes to the door.)

MOTHER. Goodbye, darling, be very happy. I'm going to bed. I
don't want to be a witness to your perdition.

(MOTHER goes.
CAV goes to the balcony and looks out.
He puts out the light. He thinks for a long time still looking
into the street.
He goes to the doll he kissed when he first came in and kisses
it again. He fondles it: he goes to the balcony again and looks
out. He flicks the lights three times leaving them out at the
end.
He leans against the wall and groans.
A discreet knock at the door.
He dries his tears. He takes a long look in the mirror and
laughs.
Another knock at the door.
He opens. SIL enters.)

SIL. I thought you'd forgotten me!

CAV. (Gently) Don't say anything yet.

(Long silence)

CAV. (Almost lyrical) Sit here where I can see you.

(SIL sits on a very low chair.)

CAV. Will you allow me to comb you?

SIL. That would be nice!

CAV. Don't say anything to me. (Still gently) Don't break the spell.
Just nod your head when you want to answer.

(He goes

(He combs her hair very carefully.)

CAV.   Am I doing it properly?

(SIL nods)

CAV.   I called you because I wanted to comb your hair.

(He draws all her hair back so that from the front she looks
like a man.)

CAV.   May I wipe off your lipstick?

(She nods.
He wipes the lipstick off with a handkerchief.)

CAV.   I've got a present for you.

(He goes to the chest of drawers takes out a little coffin places
it in her lap and puts her hands on top of it.)

CAV.   Don't move, please. Let me transform you as I please.

(He pushes up her skirt. He studies her from a distance to
guage the effect. He tries to "compose a picture".

CAV.   I don't like that necklace you're wearing. May I put another
one on you?

(She nods.
He takes off the necklace. He gets another from the chest
of drawers. It is made of nails.)

CAV.   Look over there.

(She does so. She is in profile. He looks at her.)

CAV.   Oh, that bun.

(He goes to the chest of drawers and takes out a man's wig.
He puts in on her head. She looks like a man. He takes off
her earrings.)

CAV.   Yes, that's better.

(He looks at her guaging the effect.)

CAV.   That frock doesn't suit you.

164

(He takes her frock off with great care. He puts on a sort
of mauve tunic with a thick rope instead of a belt. She lets
him do what he wants offering no resistance.)

CAV. No, that coffin doesn't suit you.

(He changes the coffin for a kind of reed which he puts in her
hands.)

CAV. That necklace doesn't suit you either.

(He takes it off and puts it on her head like a crown of thorns.
She can't help crying out.)

CAV. (Sweetly) Did I hurt you?

(She shakes her head and smiles.)

CAV. Ah! The shoes.

(He carefully takes off her high heeled shoes and her stockings
and puts sandals on her feet.
He looks at her in a state of ecstasy.
He looks at her with enthusiasm.)

CAV. How pretty!

(He looks at her from every angle.)

CAV. May I kiss you?

(She nods. He goes up to her as though he is going to kiss
her. He stops before he reaches her.)

CAV. Don't break the spell. Don't say anything. Don't say anything.

(Long silence. He looks at her.)

CAV. Let me see your tongue.

(She opens her mouth and puts her tongue out.
Very carefully he takes it between his fingers looks at it
moves it about.)

CAV. What a pretty little tongue!

(He examines her ears minutely. He looks at her eyes and
pulls the lashes.
He does it all very delicately. He leans towards her mouth.)

165

CAV.   Say a word for me. Just a minute! Careful now. For instance say - slowly - vo-lu-bi-lis.

SIL.   (As he watches her mouth close to) Vo-lu-bi-lis.

CAV.   Now say yes.

SIL.   Yes.

CAV.   Now say vo-lu-bi-lis again.

SIL.   Vo-lu-bi-lis.

CAV.   How beautiful.

(He walks round her examining her from all angles.)

CAV.   Don't move.

(He climbs onto the wardrobe.)

CAV.   (From up top) Walk around the room a bit, but don't look at me.

(She walks round the room.)

CAV.   Don't move your hands.

(He looks at her in ecstasy.)

CAV.   Now sit down.

(She sits down.
He comes down from the wardrobe.)

CAV.   Can I walk on you?

(She agrees)

CAV.   Stretch out on the floor.

(She does so: He walks on her.)

CAV.   Am I hurting you?

(She shakes her head.
He seems quite excited.
He helps her to get up.
He sits down beside her.)

CAV. Tell me, are you feeling all right?

(She nods.)

CAV. Talk to me now .... but not too much.

SIL. Yes.

CAV. Are you sorry you came?

SIL. No.

CAV. Look, I want to show you my plan will work.

(He gets out a small pram with a large chain trailing on the the ground. He pushes it up to her.)

CAV. Let me see if you can get in it?

(She gets into the pram.
CAVANOSA pushes it round the room several times.)

CAV. You're not paralysed. What a pity!

SIL. Do you mind?

CAV. It'd be easier to push you about.

SIL. I'll let you push me about any way you like.

CAV. You just don't understand. (Dreamily) And I'll show your thighs to all the men that pass by.

(Lifts up her tunic.)

CAV. What would you do for me?

SIL. Anything.

CAV. For instance?

SIL. Well .... love you a lot.

CAV. I mean something concrete, an action.

SIL. Well ....

CAV. Hang me from the ceiling and whip me?

SIL. I couldn't.

CAV. Haven't you any ideas?

SIL. I'd buy you flowers.

CAV. Flowers?

SIL. No .... books.

CAV. (Ironic) Like ....

SIL. (Suddenly she understands: in a false voice) I'd buy you, I'd buy you a whip, a miniature coffin and a doll.

CAV. Would you?

SIL. The lot.

CAV. We'll go to some Asiatic country, all right?

SIL. Splendid.

CAV. The people there won't notice I'm a monster. We .... all the people from our part of the world .... seem ugly to them .. ..

SIL. Don't say things like that. I think you're very handsome.

CAV. I didn't hear you.

SIL. Can I get out of the pram?

CAV. Are you comfortable?

SIL. It's a bit tight.

CAV. (Tired) Get out then.

SIL. Does that upset you?

CAV. No.

(She gets out and sits on the low chair. She tries to adopt exactly the same pose as before.)

SIL. Do I look all right like this?

CAV. (Somewhere else) It's not important.

168

SIL. It is important.

CAV. Pay no attention to me.

SIL. You arranged everything like this.

CAV. Yes.

SIL. You mean I'm destroying everything?

CAV. Let me see your hands.

(He takes her hands and examines them in detail.)

CAV. Pretty wrists, just right for handcuffs.

(He looks at her ankles.)

CAV. I could put them on your ankles as well.

SIL. I could stretch out on the bed.

CAV. (Angrily) What are you suggesting?

SIL. I didn't mean to offend you.

CAV. There can only be dolls on my bed.

SIL. Yes.

CAV. Can't you see? (He shows the dolls)

SIL. Yes, they're very pretty.

CAV. Don't be such a hypocrite.

SIL. What am I supposed to say?

CAV. Tell the truth: say you're jealous of them.

SIL. Of dolls?

CAV. (Angrily) You've absolutely no . . . .

SIL. I don't understand . . . .

CAV. Don't you understand they're my friends? Isn't it obvious I could never prefer a woman to them?

SIL. I didn't know. Yes, I'm jealous then.

CAV. Which one do you want to whip or chain up. How humiliating for her!

SIL. I don't know.

CAV. Whip that one.

(He gives her a whip.)

SIL. What do I have to do?

CAV. Whip her as though you hated her.

SIL. As though I hated her.

CAV. Yes, she's the one I've been sleeping with the last few nights.

(She whips "as best she can".)

CAV. Harder, harder. Like this.

(He takes the whip and starts. He whips cruelly. He falls to the floor exhausted.)

CAV. She had to be punished.

(She mops his sweat with a towel. Police siren.)

SIL. Let's go. They'll find you.

CAV. Why?

SIL. Because you killed your mother.

CAV. I'd forgotten.

SIL. Let's go before it's too late.

CAV. That's not what I asked you.

SIL. What did you ask me?

CAV. To help me bury the body.

SIL. What?

170

CAV. You won't. You're afraid.

SIL. I'll do whatever you tell me.

CAV. I want to tell you the truth. I haven't killed my mother.

SIL. Why did you lie?

CAV. Perhaps I wanted to kill her.

SIL. You couldn't have done a thing like that.

CAV. Why not.

SIL. Because you're good, you're full of kindness.

CAV. (Furious) Don't you insult me!

(He lifts the eiderdown on the bed.
Legs appear.)

CAV. And what do you say about that?

SIL. There's a doll on your bed.

(He uncovers the bed completely.
We see the body of a beautiful woman dressed just like SIL.)

CAV. A flesh and blood doll.

(He laughs hysterically.)

SIL. What's she doing in your bed?

CAV. I killed her.

SIL. What had she done.

CAV. Spent the night with me.

(He goes to the dead woman and kisses her.
He puts her on the floor on a straw mat.)

CAV. Help me to carry the body behind the screen.

(She helps him. He puts the dead woman's sandals away
in the bedside cabinet.)

SIL. Did you kill her yourself?

171

CAV. Yes. I strangled her with my own hands.

SIL. She's got handcuffs on.

CAV. I wanted her to know she was paralysed.

SIL. Did you kill her by treachery?

CAV. She didn't try and stop me.

SIL. Poor woman.

CAV. Why poor woman?

SIL. To die like that.

CAV. What a good way to die. I mean, supposing she'd died with my hands round her just after the orgasm. What more could she ask from life?

SIL. To .... go on living.

CAV. Why? Why be so cruel? She'd been happy she'd have been unhappy afterwards. Why let her go on living?

SIL. If everybody took your point of view ....

CAV. It's more than kind. I risk my life so that woman won't be unhappy.

SIL. There are cuts on her forehead.

CAV. I made her wear a crown of thorns.

SIL. Poor woman!

CAV. Are you going to cry?

SIL. No.

CAV. Cry!

SIL. To have killed this woman ....

CAV. Do you love me?

(She is about to reply: he stops her.)

172

CAV. Wait, don't answer. Remember it's the first time I've asked you.

(She is about to reply: he stops her again.)

CAV. Don't say anything. We'll leave it for another time.

SIL. I want to tell you . . . .

CAV. Don't tell me any more about your feelings.

SIL. You can guess what they are.

CAV. Don't even give me a hint.

(They sit on the bed.)

CAV. How does a man set about seducing a woman?

SIL. I don't know, but I don't think it's difficult. I suppose you start by talking to her.

CAV. Talking? About what?

SIL. Anything. The main thing for both of them is that they shouldn't be bored.

CAV. And supposing you can't think of anything to say?

SIL. People always have something to say.

CAV. But how do you "go on from there"?

SIL. Well, I suppose the man holds her hand first of all.

CAV. Wouldn't it be better to show your penis right away.

SIL. She might get scared.

CAV. Would it scare you?

SIL. Certainly it would.

CAV. But if you hold a woman's hand and she takes it away how humiliating it is.

SIL. Why think of things like that? More than likely nothing'll happen . . . .

173

CAV. And what happens after you're holding hands?

SIL. What a question! Well, the man caresses the woman.

CAV. What does he caress?

SIL. Her hands, her shoulders, her waist.

CAV. And if she refuses?

SIL. Why wouldn't she say no earlier?

CAV. So .... if a woman lets you hold her hand the rest follows quite naturally?

SIL. Yes, quite often.

CAV. That's all you have to do?

SIL. Then it's advisable to kiss her.

CAV. On the forehead?

SIL. If you like.

CAV. What were you thinking of?

SIL. I was thinking of a kiss on the lips.

CAV. Like that, point blank.

SIL. Things have made sufficient progress. Yes.

(He is nervous.
After several attempts she takes his hand.)

CAV. You took my hand.

SIL. I'm happy that way.

(They talk, holding hands.)

CAV. You're caressing my arm.

SIL. (In ecstasy) I'm very happy.

(She takes him in her arms without kissing him.)

CAV. Tell me the truth, do you love me?

174

SIL. Yes, madly.

CAV. Are you in love with me?

SIL. Yes.

(She hugs him fiercely and tries to kiss him.)

CAV. Tell me again you're happy.

SIL. I've never been so happy.

CAV. Well ....

SIL. What?

CAV. .... if you're happy I'm going to kill you.

(She takes his head and kisses him passionately.)

SIL. Kill me now.

CAV. Are you ready to die?

SIL. Yes.

(She lies down on the bed.)

SIL. Lie on me.

(He thinks. He accepts.)

SIL. I'm very happy.

CAV. I couldn't ....

SIL. I'm yours.

CAV. "You'll be mine for ever".

SIL. Whip me.

CAV. Not yet.

SIL. Tie me up. Put the handcuffs on.

(He takes the handcuffs from the bedside cabinet and puts them on her.)

SIL. Tie my feet. Whip me.

CAV. Not yet.

SIL. I love you, I love you.

(She takes him in her arms. She is "wild with passion".)

CAV. Are you ready?

SIL. Yes. (Pause) Tell me you'll remember me.

CAV. No, I'll never think of you again.

SIL. But tonight at least you'll think only of me.

CAV. I don't know.

SIL. And tomorrow?

CAV. Tomorrow I'll find another woman.

SIL. Like me.

CAV. Like last night and the one before, like every night.

SIL. I'm just today's victim.

CAV. That's the way it always is.

SIL. I want to die. Put your hands round my neck.

(He does so.)

SIL. Squeeze hard.

CAV. Is there anything you would like first.

SIL. To kiss you.

CAV. They all ask the same thing.

SIL. I'll be like the others, just one among many.

(She kisses him.)

CAV. It's time.

176

SIL. Let me kiss the hands that are going to kill me.

(She kisses his hands.)

SIL. Now, put them round my neck.

(He does so.)

SIL. Squeeze. Hurt me. Harder. Hurt me. (Shouting) Yes, yes, harder, harder. Kill me, kill me.

(She groans.
He squeezes harder.
She can't speak. He squeezes.
At that moment loud knockings on the front door and the curtain falls.)

CURTAIN

ACT TWO

Scene One

(A few moments later.
The situation has not changed.
Knocking at the door. CAVANOSA has his hands round SIL's throat.
He straightens up and looks all round to "try and understand".)

CAV. (Murmurs) Mummy, mummy!

(More knocking at the door.
CAVANOSA goes to the door. He opens it.
The LOVER enters, furious.)

LOVER. What have you done to her?

CAV. (Calmly) Killed her.

LOVER. You're mad, stark staring mad!

(The LOVER goes to SIL and takes her in his arms - she seems to be dead. He slaps her face. She appears to come back to life. She starts to breathe. She opens her eyes.)

LOVER. It's me, don't be frightened. I'll look after you, I'll protect you from this poor madman.

(Slouched in an armchair CAVANOSA seems to say something which we cannot hear.)

LOVER. Take these handcuffs off her!

(CAVANOSA is like someone on the periphery of events. He is half in a dream world. He is in a mood of self abasement and has no wish to take part in "polite conversation". He seems weary.)

178

CAV. "How am I supposed to take them off"?

LOVER. Don't try my patience. Take them off!

CAV. (Very humbly) "As you wish".

(He gets the keys and gives them to the LOVER who tries to use them.)

LOVER. These keys won't unlock them.

CAV. "I'm sorry, they're the keys to (Little giggle) to my safe."

LOVER. A fine time to start playing jokes.

CAV. "I'm sorry but I really want to laugh".

(He makes an effort to restrain himself.)

LOVER. Well, give me the keys, what are you waiting for?

CAV. (Laughs, tries to surpress it but can't. Gives him the keys) "Here". (Laughs) "I'm sorry but I really can't help myself."

(The LOVER takes the handcuffs off SIL. She slowly comes back to life.)

LOVER. Did you put this hat on her head?

(Throws down the crown of thorns.)

CAV. "It's not a hat it's a crown of thorns."

(He goes to pick it up, clutches it lovingly and puts it on a cushion.)

CAV. "Don't you think it's lovely."

LOVER. I'm not a madman, like you.

MOTHER'S VOICE. Darling, are they insulting you?

LOVER. Who said that?

CAV. "Just one of my mistresses."

LOVER. You really are revolting!

(SIL regains complete consciousness.)

179

SIL. It hurts. (She rubs her neck.)

LOVER. Don't be afraid. I'm here.

SIL. What are you doing here?

LOVER. I thought something might happen to you so I followed
you. I'm sorry.

CAV. "A gentleman doesn't follow young ladies."

LOVER. Shut up!

CAV. "When would he? Where? Explain."

(The LOVER comforts SIL.
CAVANOSA goes down on all fours by the LOVER and keeps
quite still.)

LOVER. What are you doing down there?

CAV. "At your service. I'm a donkey. Sit on me."

LOVER. The poor man's mad!

(CAVANOSA gets up.)

CAV. "Who is this young lady?"

LOVER. Don't pretend to be more mad than you really are.

CAV. "Yes, I do know this young lady, or I should."

SIL. I was very happy.

CAV. (To the LOVER) "Did you hear that? 'I was very happy.'"

SIL. I was very happy with you.

LOVER. He tried to kill you.

SIL. I asked him to.

CAV. (Looking) Mummy, where are you?

MOTHER'S VOICE. Don't let them insult you darling.

CAV. "Mummy, you're always leaving me alone."

180

SIL. You're not alone.

CAV. "You're not alone" .... "Do you hear her? Is she really talking or am I just imagining it? (To the LOVER) Can I offer you a sprig (Thinks) of thyme?"

LOVER. I can't breathe in this atmosphere. I can't breathe!

CAV. "Mummy where are you?"

LOVER. I must have some air.

CAV. "You're going mad."

LOVER. Don't worry, I'm not going to let myself get infected.

CAV. (To SIL) "Shall we play chess?"

SIL. I love you.

CAV. "Do you know the way the pieces move? The pawn ...."

SIL. I love you.

CAV. "How does the knight move across the board?"

LOVER. Shut up, murderer!

SIL. Don't call him a murderer.

LOVER. He's a murderer, he tried to kill you.

  (CAVANOSA goes into a series of exercises. He tries to
  stand on his head.)

SIL. I asked him to.

LOVER. Then it's only because he made you lose all sense. Everything's catching.

SIL. Love made me lose all sense.

LOVER. Come on, wake up. You're living in this world. Wake up no more time for dreaming!

CAV. (Who has succeeded in standing on his head) "Can you do this? See how difficult it is?"

LOVER. Look at him. He's grotesque.

181

MOTHER'S VOICE. Don't let them insult you, darling.

SIL. He's wonderful.

LOVER. He's mad.

SIL. He's free.

LOVER. I don't understand.

SIL. And I don't understand why you don't see things the way I do.

LOVER. Can't you see how ridiculous he is?

SIL. Open your eyes.

LOVER. You open yours. Most probably he's pretending to be mad to excuse his crime.

CAV. "Please kind sir, will you excuse my crime?"

LOVER. That's right, keep up the act, it'll get you off.

CAV. "The words you speak tell me something. It's as though I'd heard you talk before."

SIL. There's such a gulf between you.

CAV. "Mummy will you protect me?"

SIL. I'll protect you.

CAV. "When? Where? Shall we play chess?"

SIL. Teach me.

LOVER. Don't start.

SIL. I started. I knew what I was doing. I wanted to be his victim tonight. You wouldn't let me and that's why I hate you.

LOVER. I saved your life.

SIL. You stopped me from being happy.

LOVER. Happy when you're dead?

SIL. I'd have died at his hands, like all the others.

LOVER. How do you mean, like all the others?

SIL. Every night he seduces a woman and kills her at the height of passion.

LOVER. Don't be taken in by all his lying stories.

SIL. What lies?

LOVER. He doesn't kill a woman every night.

SIL. Lies, are they? All right, I'll show you the body of his last victim.

LOVER. Does he keep bodies "in his drawer" too?

SIL. Only behind the screen.

LOVER. Really?

SIL. Go and look.

(The LOVER goes to the screen and removes it. There is nothing behind.)

SIL. (Anxious and surprised) What's it mean?

CAV. (Distrait) "Meaning, meaning, meant. Shall I sing it for you? Shall we all sing it together?"

LOVER. Was that his proof?

SIL. I don't understand.

LOVER. Why? It's quite obvious. Let's drop the subject.

SIL. I put it there. I'm not mad.

LOVER. I'll forgive you.

SIL. There's nothing to forgive. I carried it. I saw him take her sandals off and put them in this drawer.

LOVER. You persist in this story?

SIL. Look.

(She runs to the bedside cabinet and opens the drawer. Stupefaction.)

LOVER. They're not there either?

SIL. It can't be.

LOVER. You've had a worrying evening.

SIL. (To CAV) Please tell him it's true.

CAV. "True? What does that mean, true?"

SIL. Please tell him there was a woman behind that screen.

CAV. "Should I help you?"

SIL. Just tell the truth.

CAV. "Suppose we played chess."

MOTHER'S VOICE. Don't let them insult you darling.

CAV. "Why are they always insulting me, mummy?"

LOVER. Nobody's insulted you. We all feel sorry for you.

SIL. (To CAV) Please, let's go away in the little pram. Chain me up and let's go. We'll travel the world.

CAV. "In what kind of vehicle?"

SIL. In a pram.

CAV. "Let me think now .... that'd be very slow. Don't you think a convertible would be a better idea?"

SIL. He despises me. He despises us all. You don't really want to talk to me do you?

CAV. "Yes, let's talk, let's talk."

SIL. I behaved so badly to you.

LOVER. Don't grovel like that. You disgust me.

SIL. I interrupted the ceremony, didn't I? I'm not fit to share your dream of the heights of passion.

LOVER. I wonder why I came here.

SIL. Shut up!

184

CAV. "Mummy, where are you hiding?"

(He looks for her.)

LOVER. You see, he doesn't need a woman, it's a mother he wants.

CAV. (To the LOVER) "Shall we play chess?"

LOVER. Why don't you tell me what's really in your mind?

CAV. "I must discuss something with you? Discuss or talk about something?"

LOVER. (Conciliatory) I admit I was a little short with you. But you must understand my point of view, I thought you were going to kill her. But I should like to know what you're thinking and why you behave the way you do. I'm not talking only about now, but about always.

CAV. "So, we're to talk and not play chess?"

LOVER. Believe me I'm speaking quite seriously. I'd even like to help you, if possible.

CAV. (Sincere tone) Thank you very much.

(Filled with sincere humility he kisses the LOVER's hands.)

LOVER. Please, please, let's keep this within bounds, unless this is another one of your jokes.

CAV. No, it's not a joke. Do you know something? I dreamed about you yesterday . . . .

LOVER. You've already told me your dream, remember?

CAV. Can I tell you a second time?

LOVER. I know it already.

CAV. There might be some quite radical transformations.

LOVER. Are you making fun of me?

CAV. You'll soon see. (In another tone) Mummy, may I speak? (Long silence) It's something that fills me with amazement . . . . I dream . . . . for instance . . . . Yes, here's a typical example. I dream that people are making fun of me,

185

helpless with laughter, and it seems to me that they are waiting for some kind of catastrophe to overtake me. I keep on walking and the people go on laughing, louder and louder. And I can hear some of them choking and saying "The monster's going to kill himself" but I don't understand how I'm going to kill myself and I go on walking until I come to the edge of a dangerous precipice.

(Long silence)

LOVER. I don't see why you're telling me this dream.

CAV. There's something incomprehensible about it.

LOVER. Dreams are always incomprehensible. Everybody's imagination wanders.

CAV. In that case it's not mine that wanders. I dream that people are laughing and they know I'm going to kill myself. But I don't know why. I only find out at the end of the dream. So those people who were laughing weren't a figment of my imagination because they know something I only discovered later!

LOVER. (Snobbishly) How interesting.

CAV. "How interesting!"

LOVER. I mean I understand your problem. It's worrying to think that someone else is dictating your dream to you and you're their victim!

CAV. I'd be more than relieved if they would dictate them! At last, someone who would take the bother to create my dreams and make me happy by inventing quite hair-raising stories!

LOVER. That's a quite different point of view.

CAV. I don't think so. The most probable thing is .... "Mummy did you put any sugar in my coffee?"

MOTHER'S VOICE. Yes, darling.

LOVER. (Who would like to understand) The problem you have stated ....

(CAVANOSA gets down on all fours.)

CAV. "And now, since we've got onto th~ ~ ~ ~ ~

186

subjects, please sit on my back."

LOVER. Kindly don't start again.

CAV. "Please, just once, just for a minute and I'll do anything you want."

LOVER. I never heard such a thing!

CAV. "It's the only thing I've asked you to do, and the only thing I will ever ask of you."

LOVER. (Totally bewildered) All right.

(He sits clumsily on CAVANOSA.)

LOVER. That's enough.

CAV. Please, just a little longer.

(CAVANOSA throws the LOVER to the ground in a swift movement. He jumps on him. Pins him down and puts a judo hold on his legs.
The LOVER tries to get free.
CAVANOSA tightens the holds and the LOVER cries out.)

CAV. It's a judo hold. The more you move the more it'll hurt.

LOVER. You're hurting me. You're mad.

(Yells)

CAV. Quiet now.

LOVER. Let me go!

CAV. I hadn't thought of that. (To SIL) Please, the handcuffs on the bedside cabinet. Put them on him.

LOVER. Don't do it, he might kill me.

(She goes to put the handcuffs on him.)

CAV. Tie him to the bedpost.

(SIL puts the handcuffs on the LOVER.)

MOTHER'S VOICE. Darling, don't get so excited!

CAV. Mummy, come and see me in here.

MOTHER'S VOICE. I'm just a poor old woman. What good would I be with you?

CAV. Come in, mummy.

(MOTHER enters.)

CAV. Mummy! (Kisses her)

MOTHER. Don't kiss me, darling. I'm nothing.

(MOTHER goes into a corner and begins to play cards as at the beginning of the second act.
CAVANOSA helps her, coaxing her.)

MOTHER. Why were they insulting you?

(He sits at her feet and she strokes his hair.)

CAV. They don't like me, mummy. They make fun of me. They think I'm a monster.

MOTHER. My poor darling, everyone's against you.

CAV. Everyone, mummy, just like at school.

MOTHER. Why are all these people here at this time of night?

CAV. They came to insult me.

MOTHER. That girl? What's she doing here?

CAV. Don't worry. Soon we'll be alone, just the two of us.

MOTHER. We're so unhappy! So unhappy!

CAV. Yes, mummy.

MOTHER. What have you done to him?

CAV. He was insulting me all the time so I had to tie him up.

MOTHER. Quite right, darling.

CAV. Mummy, have you forgotten all the nasty things I said to you?

MOTHER. Yes, darling, of course! Night-time doesn't agree with

188

you. It sends you mad. You get all sorts of funny ideas.
It'll soon be dawn and in the daylight we'll see each other as
we really are.

(He carefully smooths his MOTHER's skirt.
He nibbles it.)

CAV. I'm your little boy.

MOTHER. Yes, you're my darling little boy.

CAV. If there'd been lots of us you'd have only loved me, wouldn't
you?

MOTHER. Only you!

CAV. I don't love anyone but you, either.

MOTHER. And what will you do tomorrow evening?

CAV. I swear today was the last time.

MOTHER. Will this woman be the last, too?

CAV. I swear.

MOTHER. You swear the same thing at dawn every morning.

CAV. But this time I mean it.

MOTHER. What's the attraction in women?

CAV. I don't know, mummy. When night comes it seems to me
they have burning eyes that want to look into mine, hands
aflame that want to hold mine, lily-white backs for me to
scourge, and sorrowful voices to mourn the death I give them.

LOVER. This nonsense has gone on long enough.

CAV. You hear that. His lordship's getting impatient.

MOTHER. Don't worry about such trifles.

LOVER. When are you going to release me? (Pause) I shall inform
the police.

CAV. He'll drag me into court.

MOTHER. Have you done anything wrong?

189

CAV. Me, mummy?

MOTHER. Of course not darling, you're goodness itself.

LOVER. Release me, please. (To SIL) The keys are there, release me.

SIL. (To CAV) Can I release him?

CAV. (To his MOTHER) Do you want me to help you with this game?

MOTHER. It's very easy now. All the aces are out.

LOVER. Why do you have to ask him? Let me go, the keys are right beside you.

SIL. Don't you think he said no?

(CAVANOSA gets up ceremoniously and goes to the LOVER.)

CAV. May I say something to you?

LOVER. Release me.

CAV. May I tell you one of my dreams?

LOVER. Release me first.

CAV. This dream .... could be interesting.

LOVER. Why ever did I come into this mad-house?

CAV. I think it might even intrigue you. Shall I tell you?

LOVER. After.

CAV. "Now, we were saying that the people I create in my dreams know things that I don't. That's right, isn't it?"

LOVER. I've had enough of this.

CAV. Now listen. The other night I dreamed about a town I don't know. I've never heard anyone talk about it and I've never seen a photo of it. I dreamed I was standing in a square surrounded by buildings in the local style. When I woke up I looked for photographs of this town in a travel book. I found the same square and the same buildings, exactly as I'd seen them.

190

LOVER. I listened to you. Now release me.

CAV. Don't you think my dream was "interesting"?

LOVER. No!

CAV. Think what it means.

LOVER. (Persuasivley) Please I'm trying to be as understanding as I can. I know the reasons why you hate me but now, I think that ....

CAV. Do I have reason to hate you?

LOVER. Of course. First because I was unable to understand the kind of world vou live in, in fact I was quite insufferable towards you. I thought you wanted to kill my friend and I called you a murderer.

CAV. Well, if there are reasons (To SIL) Get the whip and beat him.

(She goes to fetch the whip.)

LOVER. Don't do that. You're a monster.

MOTHER. Don't let them insult you, darling.

CAV. They all hate me, mummy.

(SIL stands by the LOVER doing nothing.)

MOTHER. Like the boys at school.

CAV. But then I could come and hide by you.

MOTHER. You can now.

CAV. Will you protect me against them?

MOTHER. Yes, darling.

CAV. (Shouting at SIL) What are you waiting for?

SIL. What do I have to do?

CAV. Take his jacket off and whip him.

SIL. Yes.

(She tries to take his jacket off.)

SIL. I can't get if off.

CAV. Why don't you just say you don't want to!

(Grabs the whip and throws it on the floor.)

SIL. Let's go away together.

CAV. Where?

SIL. Travel the world, as you said.

CAV. I've only got my mother.

SIL. You've got me, too.

CAV. Shall we take her with us?

SIL. Yes.

CAV. You'll both be in the pram together tied to the same chain.

SIL. It's for you to say.

(Police siren. MOTHER goes to the balcony.)

MOTHER. (Anxiously) Look, they're taking a woman's body away.

(He goes to the balcony.)

MOTHER. Is it one of yours?

CAV. Yes.

MOTHER. The one from the day before yesterday.

CAV. Yes.

MOTHER. I told you not to leave it in the cellar. Thank God it was in the one opposite!

CAV. It had to happen.

MOTHER. I don't want anything to happen to my little darling.

CAV. Go on playing cards, mummy darling.

(He sits on the chair lovingly.
MOTHER continues to play.)

LOVER. It's insufferable. Why won't you release me?

CAV. Mummy, what are we going to do with this gentleman?

MOTHER. Anything you do will be right.

CAV. Poor thing! Don't you feel sorry for him?

MOTHER. I can't get this game out.

CAV. Do you want me to help you?

MOTHER. You're so clever you'll do it right away.

SIL. Let's go.

CAV. Go? .... Release your friend.

SIL. He's not my friend.

CAV. Finally you understand.

SIL. I'd rather you did it yourself.

LOVER. That's it, say no now. Don't put yourself out.

CAV. Are you two going to have a quarrel?

SIL. I'll do whatever you order me to.

CAV. All right. I'll release him myself.

(He lets him go.)

CAV. I ought to beat you but I feel sorry for you.

MOTHER. Look at the thanks you get from him, darling.

LOVER. What a pair! Like father like son, or rather, like mother
like son.

CAV. Clear out!

LOVER. I don't need telling believe me.

.V. Clear out and take your whore with you!

193

LOVER. Don't insult people, I'm free now.

MOTHER. They'll report you.

LOVER. I'm not a copper.

MOTHER. What's he done to you, my darling boy?

CAV. "Before you go may I tell you one of my dreams?"

LOVER. I can't stay in this house a moment longer.

CAV. (On all fours) Would you sit on my back. Just for a moment.

(The LOVER looks at him angrily.)

LOVER. (To SIL) Leave with me now.

SIL. Why are you treating him like this?

LOVER. Goodbye!

(The LOVER goes.
CAVANOSA puts out several of the lights.
The secne is in half light.
We can hardly see the MOTHER in the corner.)

SIL. You must really think I'm stupid.

CAV. (Trying to be amiable) Why?

SIL. I couldn't understand you, or make you happy.

CAV. Do you really want to make me happy?

(As he speaks he strokes one of the dolls. He kisses it.)

SIL. You think I'm hateful, don't you?

CAV. No.

SIL. Tell me it's not all over between us.

CAV. What do you mean?

SIL. Shall we see each other again?

CAV. No.

CAV. No.

SIL. Never?

CAV. No.

> (Silence.
> He strokes the doll.
> He begins to dress it as he talks to SIL. Bit by bit he puts a
> wedding dress on the doll. He also puts two hair shirts, one
> round her thighs and the other round her arm.)

SIL. Won't you need another woman tomorrow night?

CAV. No.

SIL. You're breaking the habit?

CAV. Perhaps.

SIL. You aren't sure.

CAV. To tell you the truth I don't know what I'll do when night
comes.

SIL. Will you let me come and find you in the park then?

> (He does not answer.
> He dresses the doll slowly and carefully.)

SIL. Will you let me?

CAV. No.

SIL. I'll be yours to the end. No one will disturb us.

CAV. No.

SIL. Are you afraid my friend might come?

CAV. No.

SIL. Let me come and see you in the park then?

CAV. It's no longer possible.

SIL. You've taught me so much about love and death.

> (MOTHER murmurs: "Darling, Darling."

195

SIL. I can never separate them in my mind again.

CAV. You didn't go through with the ceremony. I can't imagine you participating in it.

SIL. Is it my fault?

CAV. Yes.

SIL. Don't be so cruel to me. You showed me the height of passion. I didn't ask you for anything.

(Silence. He continues dressing the doll.)

SIL. You told me you'd whip me .... and you didn't do it.

CAV. You weren't willing.

SIL. You'd sooner torture me this way.

CAV. You've got it. Now go away and forget!

SIL. I don't want to forget.

CAV. I'm going to stay here with my mother and my dolls.

SIL. I want to belong to you as well.

CAV. No.

SIL. I'll do all the dirty work. I'll be your mother's servant.

(MOTHER murmurs: "Darling, Darling.")

SIL. Ask me to belong to your mother, if you want.

CAV. (Dreamily) Sell you to my mother, or, make a present of you ....

SIL. That's right.

CAV. Would you let her take it out on you?

SIL. Yes.

CAV. It's an attractive idea. (Dreamily) You'd be shut up in my mother's room ....

SIL. Yes.

CAV. And I'd be a long away from you, for ever.

SIL. Let me have this indirect contact.

CAV. My mother will chain you up.

SIL. I'll imagine you're doing it.

CAV. She'll torture you every time she catches me caressing one of these dolls.

SIL. You'll be the master of ceremonies.

CAV. She's a cruel woman, she'll go the full limit and nothing'll stop her.

SIL. Yes.

CAV. Tell me you want to be chained up in my mother's room for ever - I never go in there, remember.

SIL. Yes, that's what I want.

CAV. We shall never see each other again.

SIL. As you wish.

CAV. The complete convulsive ceremony.

SIL. It'll be a way of belonging to you for always.

(The MOTHER murmurs: "We're so unhappy darling.")

CAV. And the day you die, we'll bury you downstairs like the others.

SIL. I don't want to be the exception.

(Silence)

CAV. Have you fallen so low?

SIL. Why?

CAV. Do you feel sorry for me?

SIL. No.

(CAVANOSA hides himself in the doll's wedding dress.)

CAV. (Very sadly) Mummy!

MOTHER. Darling, try not to suffer so much.

CAV. Can't you hear the way they're all making fun of me?

MOTHER. Yes darling, I hear.

CAV. It's not my fault mummy. I wasn't born funny like this because I wanted to be.

MOTHER. I know, darling.

CAV. She's making fun of me too, isn't she?

MOTHER. Yes, darling.

CAV. Why do you think she's pretending to love me?

MOTHER. She's a pretty girl. I expect she's had a lot of experience and wants to try everything.

CAV. I'll stay with you and my dolls.

MOTHER. Quite right.

(CAVANOSA has finished dressing the doll. He goes to his MOTHER.)

CAV. Mummy, would you like her as a present? (Pointing to SIL)

MOTHER. What would I do with her?

CAV. Chain her up in your room.

MOTHER. I'll do anything you want.

CAV. You can beat her too.

MOTHER. I'll do that, certainly.

CAV. "Come over here please."

(SIL approaches)

MOTHER. She's a pretty girl.

CAV. Like her?

MOTHER. I'll try to get used to her.

CAV. Show her your ankles.

    (SIL shows them)

CAV. Your back.

    (SIL does so)

MOTHER. Are you really giving her to me?

CAV. Yes, mummy.

MOTHER. For good?

CAV. Yes mummy.

MOTHER. On one condition though; you're not to see her again.

CAV. Of course.

SIL. I agree.

MOTHER. (Cutting in brutally) No talking in my presence, understood?

SIL. Yes.

MOTHER. Didn't you hear what I said? I told you to be quiet.

    (SIL nods)

MOTHER. We have to tame that pride of hers.

CAV. You manage that.

MOTHER. All these stuck-up little things think about is their appearance. They imagine the world owes them a living.

    (MOTHER has got quite emotional and drops the cards.)

MOTHER. Pick them up!

    (CAVANOSA goes away, turning his back to his MOTHER, and caresses the doll, covering her with all sorts of jewels. SIL picks up the cards.)

MOTHER. Quicker - on your knees. Afraid of spoiling your

stockings, miss?

(SIL finishes picking up the cards and hands them respect-
fully to the MOTHER.)

MOTHER. I shall take you to my room and listen carefully. You
will be chained up all day. At certain times of the day I
shall lengthen the chain so that you can make my bed, sweep
the room and tidy up. Understood?

(SIL nods)

MOTHER. There's no point in protesting. When I ask you a
question you will answer yes or no by signs, that's all!

(SIL nods)

MOTHER. And don't even answer by nodding your head until I've
put the question. These are my orders. As for my son, you
will do nothing for him and I order you to forget him.

(SIL turns to look at CAVANOSA.)

MOTHER. (Angrily) No goodbyes.

(She gives her a push. They both leave the room.
The doll is now fully dressed.
CAVANOSA looks at it as though in ecstasy. He walks round
her, kisses her. Takes her by the arm like a young bride.
He goes to the drawer and takes out an opera hat. He looks
at himself in the mirror.
He goes back to the doll.
We can hear SIL's groans.
He takes the doll's arm. He tries to walk forward with it
but it falls noisily. The jewels roll all over the floor.
He picks it up coaxes it, rubs its knees. Kisses it.
He takes it in his arms and carries it to the bed like a young
bride. We can still hear SIL's cries of pain. CAVANOSA sta
starts taking the jewels off the doll, very carefully. Then
he undresses it bit by bit, slowly and delicately.
More cries from SIL in the distance.
Slowly he finishes undressing the doll.
He puts it into the bed, naked. He kisses it.
He puts out all the lights.
Groans and cries of pain from SIL.
In the gloom we assume that CAVANOSA is advancing to
the bed.
Full blackout.)

Scene Two

(The following night.)

CAVANOSA'S VOICE. Mummy! Mummy!

> (The lights come up slowly.
> CAVANOSA is in the park sitting on the bench.
> Near him a child's pram. A chain comes from the wheels to
> the body of the pram.
> LYS enters. She wears pigtails.
> She sits on the bench.)

LYS. (There is great innocence in her manner of speech) Are you
waiting for someone?

CAV. Hmmm!

LYS. I'm sorry. Seeing you sitting there I wondered if you were
waiting for someone.

CAV. (Shyly) No.

> (Excessive shyness almost a caricature ....)

LYS. Were you calling your mother?

CAV. My mother? Perhaps.

LYS. Are you waiting for her?

CAV. No.

LYS. Where is she?

CAV. (Violently) What's that got to do with it! (Gently) I'm sorry,
madam.

LYS. You called me madam.

CAV. Why not?

LYS. I'm just a little girl.

CAV. You see, I'm not very well up in these things.

LYS. Don't you know the difference between a little girl and a
grown woman?

201

CAV. I've just told you, no.

LYS. I'm a bit nervous.

CAV. Why?

LYS. Because it's the first time I've ever spoken to a man.

CAV. Am I "a man"?

LYS. You're not a woman are you?

CAV. That's enough of that isn't it. Clear off!

LYS. Am I disturbing you?

CAV. Yes.

LYS. But I haven't done anything.

CAV. What are you after?

LYS. Do you want me to tell you the truth?

CAV. Yes.

LYS. Well, I've got away from the house for a few moments. I wanted to know a man, to find out how he talks and what he says - and I met you. Let me be your friend. I'll tell you my secrets and you'll tell me yours.

CAV. Aren't you tired of telling me lies?

LYS. It's true, honestly. I took an enormous risk. If my mother finds out there'll be trouble! She keeps me locked up in her room and at night she ties my ankle to her with this rope so I won't get away. I cut it.

(She shows her ankle.)

CAV. "Are you so awful?"

LYS. She says I'm going out to meet men and she never lets me out of the house. In the mornings she's afraid I might have got out in spite of everything so she sniffs me between the legs. I don't know why? Do you?

CAV. How should I?

202

LYS. Do you think she'll notice tonight?

CAV. If she wakes up . . . .

LYS. I thought of that . . . . She'll give me such a beating!

CAV. "You deserve it."

LYS. I've done wrong haven't I?

CAV. "Yes."

LYS. (Beside herself with joy) Oh it's so nice to talk to a man. I like it very much.

CAV. Haven't you ever seen one?

LYS. Up till I was six, when I took my first communion, my mother used to let me go to Mass with her on a sunday but after that, nothing.

CAV. How do I look to you?

(He turns grotesquely round her.)

LYS. Well, I think you're very strange.

CAV. Very strange . . . . Abnormal?

LYS. Very different.

CAV. From other men?

LYS. I can't really remember properly. I mean different from my mother. It's all very pretty.

CAV. I'm pretty?

LYS. Course. If you knew my mother you'd see what I mean. I don't mean she's ugly but she's not like you. What I like are the hairs on your arm. They shine.

CAV. Do I remind you of your father?

LYS. I never knew him. But you're not as old as my mother. She's got a lot of white hairs. She has dresses right down to her ankles and she's always in black.

CAV. What do you do all day?

203

LYS. We paint big dolls, very big ones. The house is full of them. They bring a whole pile to my mother in the morning and we have to paint the lips and cheeks to make them prettier. Then in the evening they come and take them away.

CAV. Can you paint?

LYS. No, but it's very easy. You put a little colour where they tell you and that's it. It's always the same. Sometimes we have to stay up till dawn. We do it very fast. Other times we do whips and drums.

CAV. Can I stroke your knees?

LYS. Yes.

(He strokes her knees.)

LYS. Oh, I like that! If you like I'll stroke yours.

CAV. No.

LYS. It's nice being with you!

CAV. I want you to know that I am not a man as other men are.

LYS. My mother promised me that one day if I'm good she'll take me to church on Christmas Day. And I've always thought it'll be a smashing day because a man'll come and sit down beside me and I'll be able to look at him close too just as I'm doing now with you.

CAV. "Haven't you ever been good?"

LYS. No.

CAV. "What do you do wrong?"

LYS. Everything. My mother's always cross. I don't obey her and I don't do the things she tells me exactly the way she wants me to do them, not as fast as she wants. But I do my best.

CAV. As for instance when you give her the slip and come out.

LYS. Oh, yes, that's very serious. I'll get such a beating if she finds out! I know I'm not very nice. But I'm so curious ....

CAV. Will she beat you?

204

LYS. Yes. She's terrible about things like that.

CAV. Do you love your mother?

LYS. Yes. She's good to me and she looks after me. Besides she says she does it all for my own good.

CAV. I'm going to put a proposition to you. Would you help me?

LYS. Course.

CAV. Unconditionally?

LYS. Yes.

CAV. Well, I want you to kill my mother.

LYS. Your mother .... me?

CAV. Yes. I've tried several times but I've never been able.

LYS. I wouldn't know how.

CAV. I'd give you a weapon.

LYS. All right but I'll be scared.

CAV. Just for an instant then it'll be all over.

LYS. If it's that easy ....

CAV. Couldn't be easier.

LYS. What if my mother finds out?

CAV. How could she?

LYS. Well, it's going to be very interesting.

CAV. It certainly is.

LYS. Tell me, are you married?

CAV. No.

LYS. No?

CAV. No.

LYS. Why not?

CAV. Because I'm not like other people. I'm grotesque and monstrous.

LYS. Because you want to kill your mother?

CAV. Because of the way I look.

LYS. But you're a very nice person.

CAV. It's not a question of being nice.

LYS. And you are very handsome. More handsome than my mother or me, for sure.

CAV. When you get to know other men you'll understand.

LYS. That'll be very amusing!

CAV. Did you fall in love with your history teacher?

LYS. I've never been to school. My mother taught me to read and write. I know a few poems by heart and a few fables and stories.

CAV. Don't you think you've told enough lies?

LYS. Me, lie? It's the truth .... I wrote a few fables myself. I made up a story, too. Would you like to hear it.

(Silence. He is in a bad mood.)

LYS. It's the story of a little girl who's always kept locked up, and her mother chains her to the wall so that she can't get out at night. One night she escapes, she goes to the park and she meets a man. They both get into a green balloon and fly up towards the sun. Like it?

CAV. Clear out!

LYS. Why?

CAV. I told you to get going.

LYS. Didn't you like the story?

(Silence)

LYS. Shall I tell you something else?

(Silence)

LYS. I don't know how to say things people like. Shall I tell you a fable? (Silence) Shall I recite one of the poems I know by heart?

(Silence. CAVANOSA is very angry. His back is turned.)

LYS. Shall I pull faces and make you laugh? Look!

(She pulls faces. He does not look at her.)

LYS. Please, say something. Tell me to clear out, if you like, but say something.

(Silence)

LYS. Do you want me to shut up? I'll shut up if you like but let me look at you.

(Silence)

LYS. Don't you want me to look at you either? Say something to me. Say yes or no. Just nod.

(Silence. She goes to him and examines him from various angles.)

LYS. It's all so pretty.

(He pushes her away violently when she comes too near. She falls she starts to cry. Then she sits on the bench some way away from him, giving a little groan from time to time. She dries her tears with a handkerchief. She blows her nose.)

LYS. (As though talking to herself) I'm useless. This gentleman saw that, so there's an end of it.

CAV. When are you going to clear out of it?

LYS. So you'll talk to me then?

CAV. Didn't you hear me? I told you to go. I don't want to see you any more. (Shouts) I don't want to see you any more!

LYS. All I want is for you not to get angry.

207

CAV. Well you can get what you want very easily. If you don't want me to get angry just go, and don't come back.

LYS. (Almost in tears) All right. I'm going.

(She starts to go. She turns round and looks at him.)

LYS. Goodbye. And thank you!

(She goes.
Full blackout.)

CAVANOSA'S VOICE. Mummy, mummy!

(Police siren.)

Scene Three

(One hour later.
Lights come up slowly.
CAVANOSA is sitting on the bench beside the little pram.
LYS enters. She approaches the bench. Frightened.
CAVANOSA is sleeping. She looks at him for a long time.)

CAV. (He is dreaming) Mummy, mummy! (Furious) What are you doing here?

LYS. I came because I wanted . . . .

CAV. Didn't you hear what I said? Clear off!

LYS. Please . . . .

CAV. There's no please about it.

LYS. I don't want to annoy you.

CAV. You're certainly succeeding.

LYS. Let me stay here at your feet like a dog.

CAV. You've tired yourself out looking for other men and because you can't find any at this time of night you've come back to me.

LYS. No, I went to get a present for you.

(She takes a whip from under her skirt.)

LYS. Take this whip, it's for you, from me.

CAV. What am I supposed to do with it?

LYS. Whip me.

(He looks at the present, touched.)

LYS. I wasn't nice to you. I deserve it.

CAV. Yes.

(She starts to take off her blouse.)

CAV. What are you doing?

LYS. Taking off my blouse.

CAV. Why?

LYS. So you can whip me.

CAV. Leave it for another time.

LYS. You've forgiven me?

CAV. All right.

LYS. We'll be friends?

CAV. A bit.

LYS. A bit .... but for always?

CAV. We'll see.

LYS. I'm so happy!

CAV. Don't start being too overjoyed.

LYS. Can I say something to you?

CAV. Go ahead.

LYS. You won't call me stupid?

CAV. Tell me what it is.

LYS. Well, I thought I could leave home for good and come and

209

come and live with you. And I'll make certain things for you in the pram, so it won't cost you anything - whips, dolls, drums .... and all the things my mother taught me. What do you say?

CAV. I ....

LYS. And when we meet men along the way you can lift my skirt and show them my thighs.

CAV. Tell me, do you love me?

LYS. Oh, yes, a lot! A lot more than my mother and all the other people.

CAV. But you don't know anybody.

LYS. Doesn't matter, I can imagine what they're like. Anyway, you'd tie me up. I wouldn't be able to escape.

CAV. You could break the rope the way you did with your mother.

LYS. It's a chain. I won't be able to break that.

CAV. You'll get tired of it.

LYS. No I won't, you'll see. And you could do like my mother. Sniff me between the legs in the morning.

CAV. I've got someone in the pram already.

LYS. Are you going on a trip together?

CAV. Yes.

LYS. When are you going?

CAV. Today, I hope.

LYS. You're not certain?

CAV. I might as well tell you it's an old idea of mine that I've decided to put into execution.

LYS. Have you had it long?

CAV. Years I think.

LYS. I'll go back home.

CAV. And forget me.

LYS. I'll remember you. And if I ever dare slip out again I'll come back here and make a pile of stones as a remembrance.

CAV. I'll take your whip with me on the trip. I'll think of you every time I use it.

LYS. You're terrific. Are you going on a long trip?

CAV. Yes. We'll go through country after country changing towns all the time.

LYS. How lovely! So you're not going to kill your mother?

CAV. I shall never see her again.

LYS. Can I look? (She points to the pram.)

CAV. Yes.

(She goes to the pram looks under the hood and seems full of enthusiasm.)

LYS. Oh she's pretty!

CAV. Really.

LYS. She's, she's the prettiest.

CAV. That's what I think.

LYS. Now I can understand why you'd rather have her.

CAV. It's not because I'd rather have her but because I've got used to the idea of going away with her.

LYS. Makes me envious.

CAV. You'll meet another man.

LYS. I'm sure he won't be like you.

CAV. He'll take you on a trip too.

LYS. But I'd got used to the idea of it being you. I thought about it as I came back. I imagined how lovely it would be. We could make up little songs. I'd sing them and you'd accompany me on the drum.

211

CAV. Very badly.

LYS. They're very easy songs. All you'd have to do is rum-ti-ti-rum-ti-ti-tum. I can make drums, too.

CAV. We'll never see each other again. I can tell you one thing though, I like your company.

LYS. I like yours.

CAV. That's why it's better if we don't go away together. Anything marvellous would soon fade.

LYS. No.

CAV. "It's always the same."

LYS. Why?

CAV. Because later I'd want to kill you.

LYS. We could die together.

CAV. I'd just kill <u>you</u> - that's not the same.

LYS. Why?

CAV. "Out of love."

LYS. Then it'd be very beautiful.

CAV. It's no good you're starting again. You're not like the others.

LYS. I'm uglier.

CAV. You're different. I want to cuddle and kiss you.

LYS. Kiss me, cuddle me!

CAV. Hasn't anyone ever kissed you?

LYS. Yes, my mother.

CAV. Nobody else?

LYS. When I was small and my mother used to let me go to church the priest used to kiss me too. He used to take photographs of me without any clothes on and he used to cuddle me.

212

CAV. I'll kiss your knees before you go.

(He kisses her knees.)

LYS. Do you want to kiss them again?

CAV. No!

LYS. Can I kiss yours?

CAV. No. They're not the same as yours. They'd prickle your mouth.

LYS. Let me get into the pram for a minute, just to see.

CAV. All right.

LYS. Can I take her out? (She points to something inside.)

CAV. Take it out!

(She takes a doll out. She gets into the pram.)

LYS. It's ever so comfortable. You get such a good view!

CAV. Like it?

LYS. Very much.

CAV. You can stand up if you want to.

(She stands up, touches the hood. Looks all round.)

LYS. What a pleasure it must be to have a pram like this. Can I give you a present?

CAV. What present?

LYS. I'll give you one of my pigtails so you can hang it on the hood.

(She takes out scissors to cut it.)

CAV. No, don't cut it!

LYS. I don't mind as long as it gives you pleasure.

CAV. I'd rather you kept it.

LYS. Tell me, how do you find me in comparison to the others?

CAV. Very young.

LYS. Am I uglier?

CAV. No, you're prettier.

LYS. Are you just saying that to flatter me?

CAV. No.

LYS. Can I ask you a favour?

CAV. What is it?

LYS. Can I put the chain on?

CAV. It's for the doll.

LYS. Just for a moment, to see what it looks like.

CAV. All right.

(CAVANOSA takes the chain off the doll and puts it round her ankle.)

LYS. How pretty it looks!

CAV. Doesn't it so? Can I see your back?

(She shows her back which is very white.)

LYS. Like it?

CAV. It's very white.

LYS. Want to whip me a bit just to see?

CAV. No, not now.

LYS. I'm going to see how far I can get on this chain. You don't mind do you?

CAV. No.

(LYS gets out of the pram and walks in a circle the radius of which is the length of the chain.)

LYS. I can walk quite a bit.

CAV. Yes. I'll have to shorten it.

(She gets back into the pram.)

LYS. Wheel me round once, please.

CAV. Just once.

(They go round the stage.
She is enchanted.)

LYS. Go on the trip with me! Say yes!

CAV. (Without conviction) But, what about the doll . . . .

LYS. I'll be just like her, if you want. I'll always be naked, I
won't say a word.

(CAVANOSA goes up to LYS.
He takes her face in his hands and fondles it gently. She
closes her eyes and surrenders to him. Then he kisses her.)

LYS. Take me with you?

CAV. Let's go. (Dreamily) Your eyes burn to look into my eyes,
your hands are aflame to hold mine, your back is lily-white
for me to scourge, your voice is full of sorrow for your death.

(She is beside herself with joy.
He gently pushes the little pram off left.
We hear children's laughter.
Music: possibly "Petroushka" of Stravinsky.
The doll has been left on stage.
MOTHER enters right, she anxiously looks all round.
She gets up onto the bench and shouts:)

MOTHER. Come to me, darling. Come to me. Don't leave me all
alone.

(Disappointed she murmurs to herself: "I'm so unhappy."
She takes the doll and walks off right.
Police siren.
Slow curtain.)

THE END

THE SOLEMN COMMUNION

THE SOLEMN COMMUNION was first performed in this
translation on April 28th 1970 at the Soho Lunchtime Theatre,
London, with the following cast:

GRANDMOTHER	Jean Holness
GRAND-DAUGHTER	Sammie Winmill
NECROPHILE	Howard Southern
MONKS	Ian East,
	Stuart McGuigan

The play was directed by Frederick Proud

THE SOLEMN COMMUNION
'a costume suited to his tastes'
THE NECROPHILE

(It is night.

On the stage, left, is an empty coffin two candelabra and an iron cross.

On the right is a bench with communion clothes ready for the GIRL. The dress is unbelievably baroque.

Enter the two men. They are carrying a dead woman who is completely naked. They lay her in the coffin. They kneel down and pray.

We hear a peculiar kind of whispering.

All of a sudden one of the men stops praying and looks right. The other does the same. They have a horrified look.

They suddenly close the coffin and lift it on their shoulders. They exit left, hastily, carrying the coffin.

There is a pause.

The necrophile enters right and pursues the two men. He wears a costume suited to his tastes.

He crosses the stage and exits left.

There is a pause.

The young GIRL enters. wearing only her knickers, with the GRANDMOTHER. They go towards the bench.

The old woman dresses the young girl, the communicant layer by layer with great care throughout the play)

GRANDMOTHER. It's today, my dear, the most important day of your life. The day when the Lord will deign to come down to you.

GIRL. Yes, Granny dear.

chapelet: billes de chewing-gum →

surplis →

THE SOLEMN COMMUNION
'unbelievably baroque dress'
THE COMMUNICANTE

GRANDMOTHER. There you are, a little woman already. From
now on you must show a good example to the whole world.
I've already taught you everything a woman has to know.
One day you'll be married ...

GIRL. Really?

GRANDMOTHER. Yes, my child, one day you'll be married
and you'll be the pride of your husband. There's nothing a
man appreciates so much as a good housekeeper like
yourself. You'll be a real jewel for any man. Because it's
very important that you should know, when a man gets up in
the morning, he likes to put on a very white, very well ironed
shirt, and socks without holes in them, and beautifully
pressed trousers. You'll be a real jewel to your husband.
Because you know how to iron, how to mend socks and even
how to cook. And now that you're about to receive communion, you'll become a perfect Christian. I know that you're
going to be a model housewife, aren't you, my child?

GIRL. Yes, Granny dear.

GRANDMOTHER. The most important thing is the kitchen. A
dirty kitchen makes the cleanest house into a pigsty.

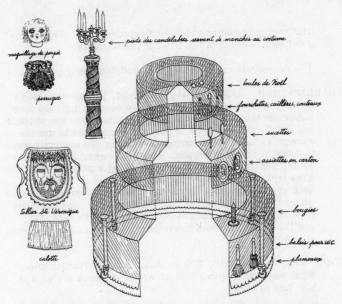

maquillage de poupée

perruque

tablier Ste Véronique

calotte

← pieds des candélabres servant de manches au costume

← boules de noël

← fourchettes, cuillères, couteaux

← sucettes

← assiettes en carton

← bougies

← balais pour w.c.

← plumeaux

I've already taught you how to put everything in order: the plates go in the sideboard, the table mats in the drawer of the cupboard, each piece where it belongs, because disorder is where dirt begins. And above all, the dishes must always be washed immediately after the meal. Nothing gives a worse impression than going into a kitchen where everything's covered with dirty plates. What's it cost you to wash up properly? A few minutes. And as for the results, you know very well how lovely my house is. But unfortunately, I'm getting old and I can't quite clean everything the way I'd like to. You understand that, don't you?

GIRL. Yes, Granny dear.

GRANDMOTHER. Men are very fussy. People say that they're not interested in things like that, but how often are household quarrels started by the wife's lack of propriety?

(The two men enter right, carrying the coffin. The GRAND-MOTHER and the GIRL stop talking and watch.

The two men cross the stage from right to left. They exit.

There is a pause.

223

The necrophile enters right and pursues them. We can see a definite swelling at the front of his trousers.

The necrophile crosses the stage and exits left)

GRANDMOTHER. And that's why, my child, you should always be very clean and very neat. As I've been saying, the most important thing is the kitchen, but all the same you mustn't neglect the other rooms. It only takes a minute to use the vacuum cleaner in the morning. You can see perfectly well that that's what I do myself, even at my age. And all the same, what with the difficulty of finding a place to live nowadays, and houses being small, it's not difficult to keep everything properly cleaned. When you go into a house where there's dust on the cupboards and the cups are dirty, it makes a terrible impression. But I'm quite sure that you'll be able to keep a house properly yourself. Won't you, my child?

GIRL. Yes, Granny dear. (She pauses. In an indifferent voice) What was that swelling just under the stomach of that man who just passed?

GRANDMOTHER. (In a cold tone of voice) That was his cock. (Pause) When the window panes are allowed to get dirty, it makes a terrible impression. And they're so easy to wash. You should wash them at least two or three times a week. It will only take a few minutes and there's no way you could use them better. All you do is take some pages of the newspaper, dip them in water, wipe the panes, and you'll see ... it's like magic. And then it's a pleasure to look out into the street. A husband never forgets things like that. I can assure you that in spite of all appearances, men care very much about these little details. You're still too much of a little girl to be able to understand all the things that men are capable of. Most of the time when a husband leaves his wife, it's neither more nor less than because he doesn't have a clean, properly arranged hallway waiting for him, such as he always dreams of finding on his return from work. But I'm sure you're going to be just like me in these matters.

GIRL. Yes, Granny dear.

GRANDMOTHER. And you mustn't forget to dust every day. It doesn't take long. You can easily pass a cloth over the furniture every morning. Only lazy drunken women have their furniture covered with dust. I remember, once when I was very young, my mother took me to a neighbour's that

224

was absolutely filthy. I passed the time by drawing a cat on the sideboard, that's how bad the dust was. How shaming it must have been for her!

(The GIRL laughs)

GRANDMOTHER. I'm quite sure you'll never be like that. Your beds will always be made up with clean sheets, the bathrooms won't have nasty smells, the floors will shine, the crockery will be properly arranged, the washing up all done, the spare linen in its place, the windows clear, not a spot of dust on the furniture and all the rubbish in a paper bin. But a good housekeeper like you mustn't forget that to keep a husband you have to be a good cook. A man who finds a good meal waiting for him when he comes home will do everything his wife wants him to. Of course life is so expensive today that, naturally, you can't manage to make up lovely little dishes like in the old days, but a good housekeeper can still do miracles if she knows how to cook. You're only a little girl, but you already know how to cook. And when you get married, you'll be worth your weight in gold.

GIRL. Yes, Granny dear.

GRANDMOTHER. A woman who knows how to cook properly doesn't have to worry. Her husband will never leave her. You must never forget that.

(Enter right the two men with the coffin. They cross the stage and exit left.

There is a pause.

The necrophile enters right. A kind of snake appears between his legs. He crosses the stage from right to left and exits left)

GRANDMOTHER. You see, my dear, it's not that difficult to be a good housekeeper. Especially if you pay attention to my advice. As you can see, even I, old as I am and moving with difficulty, manage to keep my house as shining as a new penny. Believe me, there's no excuse for sloppy women. Of course we don't have fancy furniture, because it's so dear, especially just now; but I can't tolerate furniture that's dirty and covered with dust. It costs nothing to be clean. But some women are so dirty and lazy! I don't see why they aren't red with shame. If I were them, I'd never let anyone visit me. Do you understand?

225

GIRL. Of course, Granny dear. (Pause. Then in an indifferent voice that is just barely curious) Why does that man have such a big cock now?

GRANDMOTHER. (Same tone of voice) Because he's got a hard on. (There is a pause) But there's one thing that you must never put up with: a husband who smokes. There's nothing that spoils the curtains quite so much, especially if they're white. It makes them go yellow. And in the end, the walls and the whole house has a bad smell. And besides it's an unnecessary expense. My husband, your grandfather, God rest his soul (She makes the sign of the cross) had this mania, but I succeeded in curing him of it. Every time I caught him smoking I opened all the windows as wide as possible to get all the smoke out, even if it was snowing or there was a blizzard blowing. He found it so cold that he preferred to give it up little by little. From time to time, just at first, he used to go down into the cellar when he wanted to smoke a cigarette, but he had to give that up too. What do you say?

GIRL. You did quite right, Granny dear.

GRANDMOTHER. If you want to keep your floors really shining, you should always have some slippers ready for your visitors. You must never let anyone go into the dining room without slippers. In fact you're better to stay in the kitchen where you can eat and listen to the radio while you do your sewing. The dining room should remain impeccable to receive visitors on Sunday. You should put covers on all the chairs during the week. And you must be very careful of the sun. It should never shine directly on the furniture. When you have visitors you'll put flowers on the middle of the table. Will you promise to do everything just as I say?

GIRL. Yes, Granny dear.

GRANDMOTHER. If you never forget the little bits of advice that an old woman gave you, you'll end up making a happy home. You and your future husband will owe it to me, all your life.

(The two men enter right with the coffin. Immediately afterwards the necrophile follows them in pursuit. The snake which appears between his legs is now much longer.

The two men hastily drop the coffin on the ground and run off. The necrophile throws himself onto the coffin. He

226

lifts the lid. He contemplates the corpse with ecstasy.

He starts to undress himself slowly as if going through a
ritual. He hands his garments, one by one, to the
GRANDMOTHER. Then he gets into the coffin.

The GIRL and the GRANDMOTHER watch closely. The
GIRL is by now completely dressed in her communion
robes. After having watched what is going on in the coffin
for a long time the GRANDMOTHER and the GIRL steal
quietly away and exit left)

GIRL. (in a detached voice) What's he doing with the corpse?

GRANDMOTHER. He's fucking her!

(The GIRL and the GRANDMOTHER exit left. The
GRANDMOTHER's voice gradually dies out in the distance)

GRANDMOTHER'S VOICE. Today, just as soon as you receive
your first communion, you'll become a proper little
woman. The Good Lord will come down into your heart
and purify you of all sin ...

(There is a long pause. The lights dim.

The GIRL, still dressed in her communion dress enters
carrying a knife. She approaches the coffin and carefully
looks down at what is happening within. Then she repeat-
edly stabs inside it (into the body of the necrophile). The
blood stains her communion dress.

She laughs.

Red balloons rise from the coffin towards the moon)

CURTAIN

C AND B PLAYSCRIPTS

This attractive, but inexpensive series, is designed to present the work of both established and little-known playwrights. Each volume is published simultaneously in hardcover and paperback editions.

The current list includes:

* PS 1	TOM PAINE Paul Foster	*21s	+6s6d	
* PS 2	BALLS and other plays Paul Foster	*25s	+7s6d	
PS 3	THREE PLAYS (Lunchtime Concert, The Inhabitants, Coda) Olwen Wymark	*21s	+6s6d	
* PS 4	CLEARWAY Vivienne C. Welburn	*21s	+6s6d	
* PS 5	JOHNNY SO LONG and THE DRAG Vivienne C. Welburn	*25s	+8s6d	
* PS 6	SAINT HONEY and OH DAVID, ARE YOU THERE? Paul Ritchie	*25s	+10s6d	
PS 7	WHY BOURNEMOUTH? and other plays John Antrobus	*25s	+10s6d	
* PS 8	THE CARD INDEX and other plays (Gone Out, The Interrupted Act) Tadeusz Rozewicz tr. Adam Czerniawski	*25s	+10s6d	
PS 9	US Peter Brook and others	*42s	+21s0d	
* PS 10	SILENCE and THE LIE Nathalie Sarraute tr. Maria Jolas	*25s	+8s6d	
* PS 11	THE WITNESSES and other plays (The Old Woman Broods and The Funny Old Man) Tadeusz Rozewicz tr. Adam Czerniawski	*25s	+9s0d	

PS 38   VIETNAM DISCOURSE
        Peter Weiss
        tr. Geoffrey Skelton   *25s   +9s0d

* PS 39   HEIMSKRINGLA! or THE STONED
          ANGELS
          Paul Foster   *25s   +9s0d

* PS 40   JAN PALACH
          Alan Burns   *25s   +9s0d

* PS 41   HOUSE OF BONES
          Roland Dubillard
          tr. Sarah Wright   *25s   +9s0d

* PS 42   THE TREADWHEEL and
          COIL WITHOUT DREAMS
          Vivienne C. Welburn   *25s   +9s0d

  PS 43   THE NUNS
          Eduardo Manet
          tr. Robert Baldick   *25s   +9s0d

  PS 44   THE SLEEPERS DEN and
          OVER GARDENS OUT
          Peter Gill   *25s   +10s0d

                         * Hardcover   + Paperback

*   All plays marked thus are represented for dramatic
    presentation by C and B (Theatre), 18 Brewer Street
    London W1R 4AS